"Beautifully crafted…poignant…he[...] [...] of hope. In *Bethany's Calendar*, Elaine Marie Cooper lays open her mother's heart. With grace, love, stunning honesty, and welcomed moments of humor she introduced me to, and made me love and care for, her dear, vivacious daughter until her loss became my own."

— SUSAN F. CRAFT, author of *The Chamomile*

"*Bethany's Calendar* not only gives a sensitive firsthand view of losing a beloved daughter to brain cancer, it is a practical guide for information, inspiration, and advice."

— NANCY JILL THAMES, author of *The Long Trip Home*

"Cooper never falters to truthfully report the realistic demands of caregiving and the despair she often battles. She continues to underscore the importance of dealing with the reality of terminal illness while acknowledging that miracles do still happen. It is the miracle of Bethany's life and God's role in it that Cooper seeks to emphasize and within *Bethany's Calendar*, she has managed to voice the treasure of Bethany even while dealing with her own grief."

— RJ THESMAN, author of *The Unraveling of Reverend G*
and the *Life at Cove Creek Series*

"Baring her soul with this beautiful narrative of the painful loss of her child, Elaine Cooper offers comfort and help to those who walk such a horrific path. It is a must read for everyone, giving priceless insight into this difficult journey."

— SHARON [...] [...]r of *Generations*

Bethany's Calendar

When God has other plans...

ELAINE MARIE COOPER

BREWSTER, KANSAS USA

This book is dedicated to Bethany, who has left all who knew her with a legacy of love, compassion, faith and humor. She will always be missed, this side of heaven.

Acknowledgments

I want to thank all of my friends who prayed for me during the writing of Bethany's Calendar. Your faithful intercessions on my behalf made writing this difficult manuscript bearable. While I know the Lord assured my heart that He would give me the strength to relive Bethany's illness as I wrote, your prayers were used to help sustain my strength. I cannot thank you enough.

Thanks to so many friends who helped us during Bethany's illness: *Sarah, Becky* and *Carl, Judy* and *Bob, Jan* and *Steve, Laura, Peggy, Bonnie* and *Phil, Joni* and *Bob, Sandi, Todd* and *Julie, Nancy and Tim,* all the *friends from William Jewell College,* all our dear friends at *Grace West Church* and *Grace Church,* and so many others. Forgive me if I fail to mention every name. Where my memory may fail me, be assured that my gratitude will never fail.

For all of Bethany's *aunts* and *uncles* and *cousins* who helped in so many ways, thank you does not seem sufficient. You were a blessing to Bethany as well as to Steve and me.

To all the *doctors* and *nurses* who worked so hard to keep Bethany alive, thank you for your dedicated care. Despite our human efforts, God has His own calendar for each of us.

To my publisher at CrossRiver Media, *Tamara Clymer,* and to my wonderful editor, *Debra Butterfield,* a thousand thanks — for believing in this book and for making the chapters so much better. I am eternally grateful.

And of course, to *Steve, Ben*, and *Nate* who made the painful journey with me. "Thanks" does not seem sufficient to express my gratitude. You made all the difference in helping me survive. I love you all.

And, as always, thanks to my Lord and Savior *Jesus Christ,* from whom all blessings flow.

Preface

This book should have been written ten years ago when the events were still freshly seared in my mind. But that's the problem — it was too fresh, too painful. It was all I could do to survive.

Even these few words that I have written so far bring tears to my eyes because allowing myself to remember this chapter in my life makes me realize that I have been unalterably changed by the events of B.C. — Before Cancer.

The disease was not discovered in my own body. It was so much worse. The cancer was found in my daughter's brain — and it destroyed my baby girl.

She was not a baby in the physical sense but, as any parent knows, even your adult child of twenty-three is still your "baby." They are always a part of you, even after they go to college and fly away from the nest you carefully prepared to see them safely to adulthood. Then, as they spread their wings, you earnestly pray that they will be joyful, happy, find the love of their life, and one day, perhaps, bless you with grandchildren. At the very least, you pray that they will outlive you.

But sometimes God has other plans…

"It's often quoted that every person dies but not every person lives. I want so much to live the life that God intends for me. I want to experience life to its absolute fullest. Someday I will meet my giant (or two), but that will only be the defining point of my life. It's not something I can prepare for or anticipate... Lord, any and all battles that come my way I am confident that I can face because You are with me. Big or small, You and You alone, are my strength and my shield. Thank You, my God."

— Diary of Bethany Jeanne Cooper, April 19, 1996

I used my bare hand to wipe the condensation from the inside of the windshield. My heart raced faster than my fingers, as they worked to give me some sight through a fogged window into the pitch dark at two o'clock in the morning.

Where is she?

My mind swirled with the confusion of the last twenty-four hours. None of it made sense. And now my daughter, Bethany, had fled into the cold January darkness, barefoot. I had no idea where she'd run or why.

Straining to see through the clouded glass, my older son Ben was in the passenger seat, craning his neck, swabbing away the moisture while blowing warm air into his hands.

"What happened?" His concern pierced through his sleepiness.

"I've no idea." My asthmatic lungs rebelled against the cold night air. They don't take kindly to me running outside into twenty-degree nighttime air. But I had no choice. I was chasing my daughter, who was intent on running outside, alone, in the middle of the night. "I don't know what's happening." In my bewildered frame of mind, I repeated my confusion.

My jumbled thoughts replayed the events of the last several days.

First, Bethany had been involved in a car accident that was her fault. Then she arrived home with terrible and unexpected news.

"I've been fired," she said, matter-of-factly.

Our jaws dropped before we could stop ourselves. "Fired?" My husband, Steve, stood speechless.

"Why?" was the only word I could manage to eke out of my stunned lips. Bethany's explanation made no sense. Things were not going well at work — that was pretty much all we gleaned from the conversation. But she had recently rented her own apartment. She had bills to pay.

What is she going to do?

Anger surged through me and I could see it on Steve's face.

How dare someone fire our capable, dependable daughter?

The ensuing hours were quiet with confusion and concern.

What is happening?

Later that evening her boss called to speak with Steve. We couldn't make sense of what he was saying, but there was obviously some problem that we could not decipher. And why would he call us?

Then he dropped a bombshell into my husband's ears. "Bethany seems disoriented. Has she ever been involved in taking drugs?"

Steve vehemently denied any drug-use — that was not Bethany, he said. We were both terrified and stunned. Yet events seemed to be spinning out of control with no answers.

We were already focused on her car accident a few days prior.

Her rental car would have to be returned to save money. With all that was happening in her life, I was forced to put my on-call nursing job on hold for a few days so I could drive her around to return the rental and get her over to her office to gather the rest of her belongings. That would be awkward, to say the least.

From spending time with her, I observed behavior that I attributed to stress. Her moods swung from flighty to depressed to downright paranoid. Taking a call on her cell phone, she had quickly hung up and started screaming that someone was tapping her phone calls. Her insistence was so believable, she even had me wondering if someone actually was listening in to her phone conversations.

And then on that night of January 8, 2002, events twisted out of control.

Early in the evening and exhausted from all that was going on, I struggled to get some rest. But I could hear her in the next room, singing to herself, tossing things around without a thought that others might be trying to sleep. My husband was still downstairs watching TV.

I got up to go see what was going on. Bethany sorted through her belongings and paced around like a cat looking for its nocturnal prowl.

"What are you doing?" I tried not to be irritated but I was spent from the events of the last few days.

"I can't sleep." Her wide eyes attested to that.

"Can you try? You must be exhausted. I know I am."

"Can you sing me my song? Like when I was little?" She grabbed my hand.

Such a strange, tight grip.

"Of course." Stirrings of concern rippled my thoughts.

It must just be stress. Maybe she needs to visit her counselor.

I tucked her into bed and snuggled her under her floral blanket as I began to sing…"Bethany, Jesus loves you, Bethany. You are our sweet new baby, and we love you so."

I repeated the verse I had sung to her off and on for the last twenty-three years. But this was the first time she had ever asked me to sing it to her.

She finally seemed to relax, and I kissed her good night. Stumbling back to my own bed, I collapsed under the covers and dropped off into a restless slumber.

What happened next still pulses shivers of dread up my spine.

I awoke to what sounded like a body falling down the steps. What actually happened was Bethany had snuck downstairs, saw her dad watching TV and, in a terrorized state of mind, she flung the front door open and ran outside. She was barefoot and the temperature had dropped to twenty degrees.

Flying down the stairs, I saw my husband's confused expression. "She ran outside! She claims I've been abusing her for years." The hurt at this out-of-the blue and horrific accusation was evident on his face. He had started to pull on her sleeve and she slipped away. He dared not run after her after she had screamed these charges at him.

I raced after her, shouting her name. She was wandering across the street and stopped at the sound of my voice.

I barely recognized her terrified look. "Bethany, come inside. It's freezing! What are you doing?"

She had stopped but seemed unsure of what to do.

"Come inside." I approached her cautiously, afraid she'd run away again.

Run away from what?

My mind reeled. She looked like a frightened child. I wrapped my arms around her.

"Let's go inside." I steered her carefully toward the door and guided her into the house.

She began to scream and was terrified if her dad got close to her. She twisted her torso and tried to escape. I carefully drew her to the floor and put my arms around her. Her legs pedaled in an odd, rhythmic fashion. I rocked her like a baby while she cried out, "My name's not Bethany, it's Elizabeth." She repeated this over and over.

By now Ben was awake and he groggily came into the room. "What's going on?" The look on his face showed how shocked he was, seeing his younger sister in such a state.

"Ben!" She reached her arm out for him as if he were a lifeline to safety. "Ben." He took her hand and held it. "Ben, I love you."

"I love you, too. What's wrong?"

"My name's not Bethany, I'm Elizabeth."

Eventually her rhythmic motions calmed and my benumbed thoughts focused on one thing — getting her to the hospital.

"Bethany, I need to go get dressed. Stay here while I do that. I'll be right down and I'll take you to the hospital so a doctor can check you, okay?"

"Okay."

I regretfully let go of my girl so I could hurry upstairs to get out of my pajamas and whisk her to the hospital. But what happened next sent the evening into overdrive and panic.

My husband told me later that she had slowly scooted across the floor, hoping he wouldn't notice, as she headed towards the front door. When he went towards her, she started to scream and ran out the door again. He raced after her but the closer he got, the more she screamed and fled into the darkness.

I heard her from upstairs and flew downstairs. "What happened?" Now I was screaming.

Ben, who had gone back to bed, was now up again and throwing his own clothes on.

I ran outside after grabbing a jacket and ran after her. That cold night air narrowed my lungs and I began coughing uncontrollably. I had enough adrenaline filling my system that it quickly subsided, but I could not find my daughter anywhere.

I raced back to the house. "I can't find her!"

We quickly decided Steve would stay home and call the police. Ben and I lunged into my car, hoping to discover her whereabouts. The cold air had the windows fogged up and I kicked on every possible outlet of the defroster but it could not work fast enough.

Straining to see, checking block after block, we searched but could not find our lost lamb.

We headed back home feeling defeated and desperate, but noticed something odd as we turned onto our block — flashing lights of a police car were in front of our house.

As we approached, we could see my husband speaking with two police officers. Steve saw my questioning look and said, "They found her."

Approaching the patrol car, I saw a young officer rubbing a scratch on his face. He had found Bethany sitting on someone's porch and when he approached her, she responded in terror. According to the officers, she had attacked the young policeman and was screaming at both of them. Expletives poured out of her mouth at them. One officer had put her in handcuffs and placed her in the back seat of his patrol car. The younger patrolman wanted to arrest her. The more experienced officer could see there was something else going on. "We'll take her to the county hospital. They have a psych ward there."

I looked at my daughter with unbelieving eyes. She had calmed down when she saw me and would have grabbed my hands except that she was handcuffed. I will never forget the look of confusion on her face nor her childlike words: "Mom? Was I bad?"

Fighting back fear of unimaginable proportion, I touched her arm. "No, you weren't bad. We're going to get you help."

Steve and I got into our vehicle and followed the officers to the hospital. After a brief verbal exchange about what had transpired, we stopped speaking. Our silence screamed a thousand questions as our hearts shook with emotional eruption. The only sound was my returning bronchospasms. I inhaled some asthma-relieving albuterol — and prayed.

Arriving at the hospital, we had to pause in the waiting area while they examined her. I was soon called back to be with her.

Her dilated eyes sought mine as she grabbed my hand with relief.

Swallowing past the lump in my throat, I managed to squeak, "Are you okay?"

"I'm so glad you're here. When I saw the nurses with their purple gloves I felt better because it reminded me of you."

I smiled bravely for her sake. The nurse came in, and we introduced ourselves.

"I'm a registered nurse," I said, "and I know that you'll need to test her for drugs. But I want you to know, I've been with her for the last twenty-four hours. I really don't think you will find anything."

The nurse smiled sympathetically. I'm sure she had heard that a thousand times before.

I stayed with Bethany while the tests were run.

The nurse came in looking surprised. "You were right. Everything was negative. No drugs."

Of course, now the question was, what *was* wrong?

A psychologist came in and introduced himself as "John." A pleasant man, he spoke with her for some time and then left.

Bethany looked at me with eyes I did not recognize. They were dark, fearful, and alien to me. "I don't think his name is John." Her voice reverberated with suspicion and distrust.

I swallowed with difficulty again. "Well, his name tag says 'John.'

So I think that's probably his name."

She shook her head. "No, it's not." She gripped my hand with an intensity and strength that can only be described as terrifying. I never knew that holding someone's hand that I love could ever be so frightening.

Lord, what is happening? This is not my daughter! Where is my daughter?

Note to self: "You will not fear the terror of the night…"
— Psalm 91:5

Note to others: What your eyes observe does not always tell the whole story. "Stop judging according to outward appearances; rather judge according to righteous judgment." — John 7:24

"Dear Diary, I love Alex. He is the person I dream of marrying. But of course dreams can't always come true. I espshly(sic) want to but I do not know (if) I can. It is not always that a girl at the age of seven meets a boy who is very nice to lots of people. I love him."

— *Bethany's Diary, July 1, 1986*

ethany Jeanne Cooper was born on December 12, 1978. She came into the world screaming her displeasure and, according to hospital protocol, was whisked away to the nursery and put under the lights for warmth and monitoring by the nurse.

Nowadays, immediate cuddling is encouraged as well as extensive bonding time with both parents. But this was the 1970s and she and I missed out on that initial mommy-time.

As I lay in my hospital bed after delivery, I could hear one baby crying her heart out, and I knew it was Bethany. I flagged down a passing nurse and said I could hear my baby crying. She assured me all babies sounded alike but I insisted it was my daughter crying. Although she was just an hour old, I already recognized my baby's voice. The nurse went to check, and returned, shaking her head in wonder.

"Well, you were right," she said. "We'll bring her out to you soon."

My baby girl and I were inseparable for the better part of two years as Bethany was the ultimate Mommy's girl. Looking back, she was on my lap so often it's a miracle I became pregnant with my third child! But by the time she was two, she seemed ready to take on the world and — watch out world — Bethany was ready to make her mark.

In the church nursery, she had all the diaper bags for the kids memorized as to which one belonged to each child. The workers were thrilled to have this pint-sized assistant helping them get the right bag for each child who was ready to leave.

While Ben was always tall, Bethany took after her great-grand-mother Martha, and was a very short toddler. What she lacked in size, however, she made up for with her "tall" personality. She was dynamic, demanding, and delightful.

Her memory was astonishing and, by age two, her daddy taught her a multiple-stanza Shel Silverstein poem about a polar bear in the refrigerator. She loved the memorizing and also the accolades she received as wide-eyed guests would grin at her amazing reci-tation. She thrived on being the center of attention and happily recited the poem on request.

Bethany devoured books much like her brother, and soon took to creating her own poetry. At age four, she could not yet write, but she recited a poem about Christmas that she made up. I wrote it down and gave her the attribution as author. It was sent out with our Christmas card that year.

She went to preschool when she had just turned five. Having a birthday in December had made her ineligible to start school the previous September.

When she finally did qualify for kindergarten, though, she knew a little too much already, by kindergarten standards. A month after school started, her teacher called me in for a meeting.

"I think we should move Bethany up to first grade." I was the typical fretting Mom at this recommendation, worried about the social ramifications and my daughter being the youngest in the class.

The seasoned and very sweet teacher reassured me that it would all work out. And it did. For years afterward, we teased Bethany that she was kicked out of kindergarten.

Even though she was the youngest in the class, Bethany still qualified for the Gifted Student program. Whatever she did, she seemed to excel.

Because she was so smart, however, socializing was sometimes an issue. She often had trouble finding compadres in her class who could appreciate her intelligence, as well as her humor.

In fifth grade she made an awesome friend named Mary, whose family was from the Philippines. She and Bethany were chums who could laugh and be both silly and smart at the same time. We were so pleased.

But that same year, Steve got a new job in Iowa and it was time for the kids to bid farewell to Southern California and their friends. The move was hardest on Ben and Bethany. Younger brother, Nate, who was in second grade, had an easier time with the transition.

It took awhile for Ben and Bethany to feel more at home in Iowa but eventually they made friends and adapted. The move was definitely the hardest on Ben, who was in middle school at the time. Life is never easy in middle school but to have a move made it even tougher.

Bethany was involved in extracurricular activities at church, and knowing what it was like to be the new kid, she made an extra effort to reach out to those who were alone. She befriended kids who others shied away from. Although super smart, she was kind to kids who were developmentally disabled and somehow found common ground with anyone and everyone.

She always struggled with feeling inadequate among the cool

kids. She was frustrated with her less-than-movie-star looks, even bemoaning her parentage in one fit of teenage angst. But as she matured, her inner grace took over and she emanated beauty and joy wherever she went.

In high school, she started a ministry of visiting the elderly in a local nursing home. She made all the phone calls and arranged for visits to the care center with the group of teens who signed up to participate. She was comfortable with everyone — there was no one she could not speak to, nor elicit a smile from. She was beautiful.

After graduating as one of the valedictorians at her high school, she was ready to head south to William Jewel College in Liberty, Missouri. It was a fairly small liberal arts school with lots of opportunities for outside education and experience. The most fortuitous circumstance came in her sophomore year when she was offered an internship in Senator John Ashcroft's office in Washington, D.C.

Almost before we could lift our jaws from the floor, we were watching Bethany take off from Kansas City airport in January of 1998, headed to D.C. She worked there all through spring semester.

What future awaited our daughter, we wondered? We knew time would reveal it, and we looked forward to an adventurous life for our only daughter.

When she was a junior in college, Bethany spent her entire school year studying at Keble College, Oxford University, in England. During this year of 1998, I learned about emailing. It's hard to believe that we were ever without such a convenient form of communication. For our family, it suddenly became a necessity for keeping in touch without spending a fortune. I was grateful to become adept at it.

Bethany came home for Christmas in between semesters. It was then I noticed something a little different. I could not put my finger on it, but there was a change — so subtle perhaps only a mom would notice. Little things like inconsideration for people — and this from a person who had previously been a master of compassion.

When she finished her second semester with excellent grades, she came home for the summer. Again I noticed a change. Going to Target with her one day, she suddenly disappeared. Poof. She had vanished.

Feeling rather silly, I eventually had to have her paged. It seemed ridiculous. She was a grown woman, after all. The most disturbing part was her complete lack of awareness for how rude her behavior was. She seemed quite put out that I was put out by her disappearance.

Perhaps she's just stressed…

Senior year of college was a bear for Bethany. She had never in her life struggled in school. She had always excelled academically no matter the challenge. Suddenly she was frustrated and upset. We thought perhaps it was the faculty advisor for her major with whom she did not get along very well. Whatever it was, we were all relieved when graduation arrived. I could sense her disappointment that all her friends received honors for their achievements while she received none. Bethany's less-than-stellar scores in senior year made her ineligible. It seemed unfair for her, after all of her successes. Yet we were thrilled she had graduated and had a wonderful celebration with her delightful college friends after the ceremony.

We moved Bethany's things home, and it seemed she could not escape from school fast enough. There was no sentiment — no regrets about leaving. It was so unlike her.

I guess she just wants to get on with life, I reasoned.

Moving back home, Bethany's intent was to find a job in Boston near where I grew up. She and her cousin Julie, who already lived there, were making plans. They were as excited as school chums.

In the meantime, I was planning a huge family reunion in Iowa, with family members coming from all over the country. Carrying out this two-day party was time-consuming and complicated, especially since I was working full time as a nurse. Bethany was a great help with the preparation, but her excitement about starting her new life in Boston is the predominant memory I have from that June of 2000.

Her joy peaked when she landed a job with a large firm right in the city itself. She and her cousin found an apartment in a nearby suburb and her life seemed to just be beginning. But after a few months of her dream life, the nightmare began — and so did the phone calls.

One call on a Saturday evening threw Steve and I into parental angst of high proportion:

"Mom, I'm lost. I can't figure out where I'm going."

I fought panic as I tried to talk her through her dilemma. These calls were becoming more frequent and alarming. Her dad and I prayed for the Lord's protection over her.

When I had gone out to see her for a short visit that fall, she seemed to be her bouncy usual self. But then anger would erupt along with a severe headache.

She lost a great deal of weight.

Her new life must be changing her eating habits, I reasoned.

But then the money problems began.

"Mom, I can't make ends meet."

Bethany had always been able to manage a budget with the skill of a master accountant.

But I knew something was seriously wrong from her voice.

"Listen to her!" I fairly yelled at Steve. "There's something very wrong."

Call it mom-sense, or just practical sense but things seemed to be falling apart for her in Boston. We suggested she come home in spring of 2001. Steve flew out there and drove Bethany and her belongings back to Iowa in her little economy car.

She was devastated and depressed. Her heart wanted to stay with her cousin and her friends from church in Massachusetts. But she couldn't manage it, and the failure completely disheartened her.

Spending long hours in her bedroom with the curtains drawn, we finally convinced her to go to counseling. Perhaps that could help.

Steve and I prayed — so fervently.

Soon, a little light seemed to shine as she spent less time in her room and more time looking for a job. She waitressed for a few months just to pay her bills. But she got her dream job working in a campaign office. Her skills gleaned through the years qualified her and, for a brief time, she thrived in the environment.

She found an apartment and began throwing gatherings for old friends and new. She was the ultimate gracious hostess. And she was loved for her humor, her wit, and her kindness.

But then, her life began to unravel again — and this time, the threads could not be repaired.

She had been fired from her job. And now she was in the emergency room at the county hospital.

Note to self: "He Himself has said, I will never leave you or forsake you. Therefore, we may boldly say: The Lord is my helper; I will not be afraid. What can man do to me?" — Hebrews 13:5-6

Note to others: Pray for wisdom in times of confusion and withhold judgment. "For now we see indistinctly, as in a mirror, but then face to face. Now I know in part, but then I will know fully, as I am fully known." — 1 Corinthians 13:12

3

"Am I becoming more sane every day or am I going crazy? In any case, I'm changing on the inside. It's like the day I looked in the mirror and said, 'Dear Lord, where did she come from?'"

— *Bethany's Diary, February 8, 1999*

They put my baby girl in the psych ward.

It was the most devastating moment in all my years of parenting. The sheer terror of admitting her to this unit cannot be described. Dozens of patients with mental illness and behavior disorders roamed the halls.

I'm leaving my daughter in hell. God help us…

What overwhelmed me the most was the fact that it was both women and men who were in this lockdown area.

Pulling the head nurse aside, I grabbed her arm. "The men and women are all together?" I'm certain the panic spilled from my words.

She assured me they were separated overnight, with a locked door in between. It was small comfort.

God, where are you? My spirit wanted to scream, but I was voiceless. The staff assured me they would watch out for her. Could I trust them?

You can trust Me. A still small voice echoed in my soul.

I wanted to believe Him. But my faith was at an all-time low. I grasped my confused daughter in a desperate hug and told her I'd be back to see her tomorrow. With weighted legs and hearts, Steve and I staggered toward the locked door where a staff member unlocked the bolt for us. The sound of the door shutting behind us echoed like a metal coffin.

Ben was waiting for us at home. What could we tell him? No one knew what was wrong. We were consumed with confusion and fear.

Ben stared at me as I made a cup of hot tea to calm my nerves. "How did you stay so calm? I wanted to scream at her," he said.

I glanced into his sad eyes. "Because I knew something was terribly wrong. I knew I needed to just hold her and comfort her."

He shook his head in bewilderment. It was uncharted territory for all of us.

I was so grateful Ben was even home. Up until recently, he had shared an apartment with two other bachelors in a nearby suburb. After September 11, our college-grad son had applied at the navy recruiting station to go into Officer's Candidate School. The images of planes smashing into the World Trade Center buildings had haunted him. "I want to do something to prevent that," he expressed to me one day. So while he awaited word from the United States Navy, he moved back home rather than renew his apartment lease.

Although it was not easy as parents, Steve and I fully supported his decision to answer the call. How could we say someone else's son should join the military, but discourage our own son from protecting our country? We had raised our kids to do their part, wherever the Lord led them. Apparently, He was leading Ben on a new venture.

Now we were facing a family crisis of even greater proportions. My parental limbs felt stretched to the breaking point.

Visiting Bethany in the psych unit the next day did little to assuage my fears. The look of terror in her eyes gripped at my mother's heart. I felt physically ill at our upside-down world of the unknown.

Counselors and nurses were as baffled as we were.

Why can't they figure out what's wrong? Everywhere I went, I wanted to scream, but my thoughts and emotions remained locked — they were as much a prisoner in my mind as my daughter was an inmate in this ward of terror.

Collapsing back at our house, with Steve and Ben both at work, I finally got a phone call from the hospital psychiatrist. I'd been trying to connect with the man to discuss Bethany and try to piece together this horrible puzzle. He was just as anxious to solve the mystery as we were.

Grasping for straws, I asked him, "Do you think the car accident she had a few days ago did something to her? Maybe she bumped her head?"

Much to his credit, the doctor immediately responded and ordered an MRI of Bethany's head. She had already been in the psych unit for four days at this point.

The results of the MRI set a new ball in motion, with an immediate transfer to a different hospital. It was a whole new ballgame that would forever change all of our lives. It was a game none of us had ever wanted to play.

Note to self. "I cry aloud to the LORD; I plead aloud to the LORD for mercy. I pour out my complaint before Him; I reveal my trouble to Him. Although my spirit is weak within me, You know my way." — Psalm 142:1-3

Note to others: Be there for friends who need you, either in prayer or in presence. "…there is a friend who stays closer than a brother." — Proverbs 18:24b

---

"There's definitely room in life for pain. It's what changes us and toughens us up and keeps us connected to reality. I don't like pain or want pain and I am not going to start asking God for more of it. But darn it, I think I need some more pain in my life...God is prompting me to make myself available and ready for both good and bad things."

— *Bethany's Diary, October 20, 1998*

*S*ee this white here? That's not supposed to be there."

The nurse pointed to the image from the MRI, now illuminated on the light board in the hospital room. Bethany had been admitted to the neurology unit, and we were awaiting the arrival of the neurosurgeon, while his nurse tried to prepare us for the results.

"Not supposed to be there?" My question was clouded by my fatigue. I was operating with little sleep and under maximum stress.

Maybe if I shake my head, it will thrust my thinking processes back in order...

The sweet nurse had a pained yet professional look on her face. She was trying to break this news gently. "We'll have to ask the doctor."

His entrance into the sterile-looking room saved the woman from revealing more than she wanted. The surgeon thrust his hand forward and shook each of our limp fingers with a sturdy grip.

He again pointed to the MRI image, detailing the mysterious

white spots that seemed to inhabit a large section of the picture.

I nodded as if in understanding, not comprehending much of what he was saying. Everyone seemed to be informed that I was a registered nurse. What no one seemed to grasp was the fact that I was not there as a nurse — I was there as Mom.

Not to mention the fact that neurology was my worst subject in physiology and clinical nurse's training.

Don't they know I hate neurology?

No one seemed to care about that as everyone explained Bethany's devastating diagnosis: "She has a brain tumor. It's likely cancerous. We'll know more when we do a brain biopsy."

A brain biopsy?

They would know more after the pathology report came back but they needed to do surgery right away so they could get started. "She will likely need chemotherapy and radiation…"

Can I run away now?

Stealing a glance at my daughter, I wasn't sure she comprehended the words he was speaking. Everything confused her. I knew I was confused and, as far as I knew, I didn't have a brain tumor. She seemed to be completely baffled.

We nodded our heads in robot like understanding.

Bethany would be having surgery first thing in the morning. Early — very early. Surviving on little sleep for the last several days, I knew I needed my strength for what was ahead.

Pulling her nurse aside — out of Bethany's hearing — I explained that I needed to get some rest but I would be back first thing in the morning to be with her. I made certain she understood Bethany's behavior was unpredictable, and they would need to watch her.

My robot-legs went back into the room while my robot-smile assured Bethany I would be back first thing in the morning to stay with her. She nodded her understanding, and we hugged. It was our first hug of comfort in this uncertain journey. I couldn't allow tears to start now. If they started now, they would never stop. I needed to be strong. For her. For Steve and the boys. For myself. If I could not be strong, I could envision my whole family falling apart at the seams. I would not let that happen.

God, please don't let that happen.

The surgeon was late for Bethany's surgery.

One by one, the patients in the pre-surgical holding area were wheeled back to their operating rooms. Not Bethany. She lay with her oversized surgical cap highlighting her wide eyes. Her IV was running. Ready. Apparently the doctor was not.

I squeezed her hand reassuringly and smothered my anger. I faked a smile. "I'll be right back."

Sauntering over to the nurse's station I noticed once again that the doctor was ridiculously late. He should have been there over an hour ago.

I smiled with bared teeth. "Where's my daughter's doctor?"

She fumbled with the phone. "I don't know." Her voice whispered. Tension creased her brow. "Let me call him."

She waited for the doctor to pick up her call, as she avoided my intense stare. Finally she hung up. "There's no answer."

"Great."

"I'm sorry. I'll keep trying." The poor woman smiled with embarrassment and sympathy.

Walking back to Bethany, I managed a weak reassurance. "I'm sure he'll be here soon."

After a few moments, the doctor called. He'd slept in. Then his cell phone fell apart when he went to answer it. He was so sorry.

I tried to be pleasant but my inner Mother Bear reared its ugly head. "Okay," I told him. Holding back my feelings as much as I was able, I informed him my daughter was waiting. Had been waiting. For awhile.

Hanging up the phone, I recalled someone telling me that my daughter's neurosurgeon was balancing his current medical practice while returning to school for an additional degree. It seemed a ridiculous load for any human to carry. Here I was staring at my daughter looking so afraid in that hospital bed waiting for brain surgery, while her over-achieving and exhausted doctor pursued his personal goals. Ripples of anger pulsed through my veins.

But I had to restrain my emotions. It would do no good to release them in front of my anxious daughter nor the distressed nurse who could not control the situation. God must have given me the strength and grace to move on.

This was to be the first of many Mother Bear moments in the next year and nine months...

Note to self: Do not let seeds of bitterness grow and flower in your soul. I soon learned that grief brings a plethora of angry moments. While it is part of the grieving process, I also learned that no matter what I'm going through, God still expects me to be holy in His sight. He gives grace but He also gives strength in the darkest moments — strength to forgive and be filled with His Spirit.

Note to others: It's all right to express discontent but it's always wise to pray before speaking. "Be angry and do not sin." — Ephesians 4:26

5

"Why must we hurt? Why must we struggle? So that we can appreciate the victory. So that we can understand mercy and grace. So that Christ can be glorified in our lives."

— *Bethany's Diary, September 24, 1996*

*S*ometimes there are moments in your life when your greatest fear has become a reality. This was one of them for me.

My daughter had brain cancer and the prognosis was terminal.

As the surgeon visited with my family and me in the waiting area, his experience had taught him the scenario was not good. The likelihood that the pathology report would confirm the rapidly growing cells to be an aggressive glioma, spreading tentacles of destruction throughout her grey matter, were high. It could be treated for a time. But would likely return. And it was impossible to remove.

Words cannot adequately describe the impact of this news on all of us: my husband, two sons, Bethany's pastor's wife who had graciously come to the waiting area, and me, Bethany's mom. My mother's heart seized with the thought. Part of me was dying.

My greatest fear had always been losing a child. God was now going to take me on that journey, and I hated it. I feared it beyond any other trial I could have envisioned.

Oddly enough, I never asked, "Why my daughter?" As a nurse, I had seen too many instances of unexpected tragedies that impacted families, losses so deep and painful that they would tear at the heart of the most hardened medical person.

But now it was my turn and I was suddenly one of those moms about to face the incredible battle against a cancer that desperately wanted to take over my daughter's brain. It wanted to destroy her. And I wanted to fight back.

I could already see Bethany had lost a few hidden battles that had occurred silently. The hints had been there in her occasional strange behaviors. But the ensuing paranoia and confusion the night she ran outside into the freezing cold were the slap-in-the-face that forced us to deal with the sting of brain damage.

Her tumor was located mostly in the right frontal lobe, an area of the brain responsible for emotions, fight-or-flight responses, and rational thinking. The site of the brain tumor had impacted her social behavior as well as her ability to interpret feedback from her environment. One study indicated that right frontal damage could be observed as pseudo psychopathic.

While there are many types of brain tumors and many locations in the brain in which they can occur, the location and spread of the disease determines the symptoms.

The destruction from Bethany's tumor on her healthy brain tissue had left permanent damage by now, and we, as a family, had to adjust our thinking as to how we could keep Bethany safe. Those who witnessed the terrible night in January wanted no repeat scenarios.

Her doctors prescribed medications to help control her symptoms, such as the paranoia and the strange seizure activity that caused her to flee into the night.

Before she got home from the hospital, we ordered a security service that would set off an alarm if the front doors opened. The goal was not to keep intruders out, but to keep our daughter safely in our home, especially in the middle of the night.

Next, I had to inform my supervisor at the school district where I substituted several days a week as school nurse, that I had to take time off. Her sympathetic reply assured me I could count on her support and that I should take off whatever time I needed. I am still grateful for her depth of understanding.

Our lives were turned upside down in so many ways. I had to take over all of Bethany's bills. Without an income of her own, and with my decreased income, it became a true financial struggle to keep up. God provided, but it was more stress in an already anxiety-filled atmosphere.

Her friends from church rallied around to help move her things out of the apartment she'd been renting and bring them back to our house. We set everything up in her new bedroom downstairs so she would be able to walk easily into her new surroundings and feel herself welcomed home while she recovered.

We were all excited the doctor had only shaved a small portion of her hair for the biopsy. If you looked closely, you could notice the lack of hair but, for the most part, her surgery was hidden. It was a plus for Bethany's self-image as she had some minor paralysis on one side of her face and limbs that would diminish with time, but caused her to struggle with eating. Foods frequently fell out of her mouth when she tried to eat. One of her wonderful friends from work, Will Rogers, visited her in the hospital and didn't mind her difficulties at all. His completely accepting presence put a lopsided grin on her face. I will always be grateful to him.

While the house was readied for Bethany's return from the hospital, the fear in those of us awaiting her arrival was in the red zone of apprehensive terror. What would it be like? What if her behavior spun out-of-control again? What if…? The questions never ended.

One day I was sitting with Ben at the dining table while we contemplated her soon homecoming. I was absentmindedly spooning gelatin into my mouth when a large red blob fell off of my face and onto my lap. I glanced at Ben and smirked. "I think I've been hanging around Bethany too much."

He laughed for the first time in days. "I needed to laugh."

Indeed, we all did. It was a moment of stress release in our new world of the terrifying unknown. I would learn to look for humor in the ensuing months and hold onto it as the gift it was.

Note to self: "A joyful heart is good medicine..." — Proverbs 17:22

Note to others: There is always something you can do to help if you are a friend in such a situation. At the very least you can pray. If you are able, fill a family's car with gasoline. Drop off a meal or a gallon of milk. Send a card. If you can visit the sick, do so. Don't wait to be asked. The only mistake you can make is to pull back and do nothing.

"I was sick and you took care of Me'... 'When did we see You sick, or in prison, and visit You?' And the King will answer them, 'I assure you: Whatever you did for one of the least of these brothers of Mine, you did for Me." — Matthew 25:36, 39-40

"Father, thank you so very, very much for the encouragers that You have given me in my life. Thank you for hands that lift me up when I am down, hearts that cheer with my victories and hurt with my sorrows."

— *Bethany's Diary, December 10, 1995*

They say bad news travels fast. This time it spurred the quickest response from Bethany's college friends, and I was in awe of their hastily created comfort in the form of a hand-made quilt.

Prompted by one of her college friends, the young ladies who had been there for my daughter throughout her college years planned the project. They pieced together over a dozen quilt squares, each unique and beautiful, to blend together into a quilt. The variety of squares was impressive and beyond beautiful: Photos of Bethany and her friends transferred onto cloth, Bible verses written out in exquisite design, an embroidered "God loves you and so do I." This tangible outpouring of their care and concern was the most precious offering of love for my daughter.

One quilt square, acknowledging Bethany's love of tea, displayed a blue teapot with a rhyming verse about taking tea with a friend. Another one, with an exquisitely drawn image of the mother of Christ holding an infant, expressed in permanent ink, "May Christ hold you in His arms as this mother must have held Him." Another square expressing the humor she shared with her pals, was embroidered, "We are all worms, but I do believe, you are a GLOW WORM!"

The embroidery skillfully wrought by one fellow co-ed seemed to sum up the situation: "Manna from heaven, abundant for today, one day at a time."

Not only did her college friends carry out this project in record time, nearly a dozen pals converged on our household one weekend as a show of support for Bethany before she began her cancer treatments. Coming from as far away as Texas and Pennsylvania, the faithful friends planned a weekend filled with activities for her with hugs and a show of caring that brought tears to my eyes more than once. The gals were never in the way. In between visits, they stayed at a nearby motel, allowing Bethany the rest she needed. They were sensitive throughout and brought soothing sunshine of support in our cloudy world.

There was another cloud that covered our household at this time: Awaiting word about Ben's future.

Prior to Bethany's diagnosis, we were at peace with our older son going into the military. Now, I wanted to beg him to stay home.

Besides awaiting news from the United States Navy as to whether or not they'd accept him into Officer's Candidate School (OCS), Ben was also waiting to hear back about a lucrative job offer.

Surely You want Ben to accept a job offer here and work close to home, Lord. I need him. Bethany needs him. Surely that's Your will, Lord. Right?

But the truth of the matter was, I had no idea what God's will for Ben was. I knew what I wanted, but I did not even pretend to know what God's will was. I knew one thing, however. Deep down,

I wanted God's best for him.

Taking a deep breath, I did something I rarely do: I threw out a fleece — asking for a sign. In Judges 6:36-40, a warrior named Gideon was unsure if God would save Israel through his hand. In desperation for an answer, he specifically prayed that if God would save Israel through his leadership, the dew would fall overnight only on a wool fleece, leaving the surrounding ground dry. This would be a sign that God was with Gideon. God answered his request.

Just like Gideon in the Old Testament, I prayed a very specific prayer, and threw out my own "fleece."

Lord, if it's Your will that Ben enter the military, then help me know it's Your will by having the navy call first. If it's Your will he accept that promising civilian job offer, then let them call first. But Lord, I need this sign from You. I need to know Your perfect will for him. Help me to know Your choice for Ben so I will feel Your peace.

I had no idea just how specific God could be in answering my prayer: The navy called Ben first — just thirty minutes prior to the call from the civilian job that would have kept him closer to home.

I knew what God was telling me, but my heart was still crushed. With Nate doing an internship six hours away in St. Louis and Ben soon heading to Florida to go to OCS, Steve and I would be waging the cancer battle here on our own. And Steve had to work fulltime. I would, for the most part, be on my own to carry this load of supporting my daughter through this nightmare.

Feelings of utter loneliness and despair encompassed me. But so did the Lord's comforting arms. Despite the terrifying situation, His promise of never leaving or forsaking me gave me that unexplainable peace that passes all understanding.

But it was a peace that would be challenged many times in the coming months.

Note to self: "Trust in the LORD with all your heart, and do not rely on your own understanding; think about Him in all your ways, and He will guide you on the right paths." — Proverbs 3:5-6

Note to others: Our greatest earthly treasures at this time were friends who brought us meals, gave us hugs, prayed for us, cried with us. Their love and show of support helped give us the strength to endure. If you have friends who are in desperate need of comfort, be the hands of Jesus to minister to their needs.

7

"I just don't worry as much about the way that I look. I'm content with the way that He made me, inside and out. My body is just a shell for the real me. I'm so thankful for the Father's voice."

— *Bethany's Diary, June 4, 1996*

*W*e didn't know what to expect that first session of chemotherapy — but in our wildest imagination we could never have anticipated a visit from a celebrity. Her abrupt and loud appearance was both unexpected and unwelcome.

It was February 13 and it had already been a tough week. Radiation treatments began the day before and it was emotionally traumatic, to say the least. While Bethany did not feel the radiation beam itself as painful, it was uncomfortable and frightening being secured to a hard table and pinned down by a stiff webbed mask created just for her. The immovable mask was necessary so the radiation beam would be directed at the heart of the tumor. Although she had bravely walked into that chamber with the assistance of the radiation tech, the look of fear in her confused eyes made my mother's heart cry.

Why, Lord?

I waited outside and prayed.

Now we were in a large, horseshoe-shaped room, which was the chemotherapy suite. Soft recliners lined the edges of the room and a few chairs were already occupied — an elderly gentleman in one, an older woman in another. Bethany was the youngster in the group.

The chemical smell of the cancer-fighting drugs was sickening to me. It was an overpowering, plastic smell that was nauseating and took my appetite away. My nose has always been ultra-sensitive to strong scents, and chemotherapy has a unique and unforgettable odor. I wish I could forget it.

Always keeping a smile plastered on my face, I helped usher Bethany towards the recliner of her choice. She chose one farther down the U-shaped area and settled in with her dad and I next to her. We came prepared with a James Herriot book that we knew would provide engrossing stories to distract her during the two-hour infusion of drugs. We tried to provide comfort and quiet during the process.

Once she seemed calm and the drip of the intravenous solution began its journey into her veins, I suggested to Steve that he grab a bite to eat. He had blood sugar issues, and I didn't want to have two patients to take care of. He offered to pick something up for me, and I gladly accepted. He left us as I read to Bethany the delightful tales about Herriot's experiences as a veterinarian in Yorkshire, England, in the 1930s. *All Creatures Great and Small* was a favorite for all of us.

Steve hadn't been gone fifteen minutes when our quiet reverie was disrupted.

The double doors of the chemotherapy suite literally burst open. My eyes were drawn to the doorway and the first thing I noticed were cameras — both video and still cameras, large enough to be used for serious picture-taking.

It was difficult to discern what was happening, but the high-pitched, sweet voice of a young woman became prominent. Introducing herself to the first patient she came to, I could hear her address the hospital-gown-clad man. Somewhere in her conversation, I picked up that she was a celebrity and that she was on a mission that year to visit with cancer patients.

Feeling my hackles rise, I tried to resume reading to Bethany. But the disruption of the visitor, not to mention the sounds of cameras clicking, were a complete distraction. I could see Bethany's eyes widen.

"Don't worry. I won't let them photograph you."

Bethany was clad in sweats and comfort wear. She had on no makeup and part of her hair was missing from the surgery. She anticipated more hair loss from both the chemo and radiation. I could practically read her already confused mind: *This beautiful woman will see me like this?*

My emotions veered from grief for my daughter to utter outrage at the situation.

How dare this woman visit my daughter at such a vulnerable time! Who had allowed this intrusion?

It was an entire entourage of hospital PR folks, cameramen, the celebrity, and her handlers.

A staff person from hospital marketing approached Bethany and me with a friendly smile. She explained the woman's presence.

"Miss (so-and-so) has decided to make visiting cancer patients her goal this year. Apparently she knows someone or has someone in her family with cancer."

Don't we all?

I glared my displeasure. "There will be no photos taken here."

The woman seemed taken aback, but responded that was fine.

No, none of this is fine.

The most ungodly thoughts went through my mind.

I'd like to take that camera and…

By the time the celebrity had arrived at Bethany's chair, I was poised like a cat ready to attack. But I also realized I did not want to make a huge scene and let my daughter's fragile emotions be overwhelmed by my anger.

The young woman with the perfect makeup and hair approached my daughter. Introducing herself, she stared with sympathy at my daughter and her voice dripped with honey. "I just want you to know that I'm thinking about you."

Really? You're thinking about my daughter? You don't even know her. Why are you here?

Tears welled in Bethany's eyes along with an expression of despair. It took all the self-control I could muster to hold my tongue. But apparently my glare was screaming volumes by the look on the young woman's face. She quickly left my daughter's side and no cameras were clicked.

I squeezed Bethany's hand and reassured her that no one took pictures of her while she felt so ill. She seemed relieved, and I squeezed her hand for reassurance. Still swallowing back my rage, I resumed my quiet reading of James Herriot as the raucous entourage accompanying the star flew out the door again. It was like watching the beautiful Glinda being whisked away in the land of Oz.

I never did care for that movie.

When Steve returned, he could hardly believe the circus he had missed. He brought me some food as promised, and I took it to the outside waiting area so the smell would not sicken Bethany. But after the scene I had just witnessed, the food lost its appeal. I was caught between nausea and anger of the highest level. Mama Bear was in full protective mode.

After the infusion of chemotherapy finished, we gathered her things and helped Bethany down the hall and back to the car. Her dad had to return to work so I drove my exhausted daughter home.

I did not bring up the scene with the celebrity after we got home. But Bethany did.

"Mom, did they take my picture? What if I'm on the news?" Her tears melted my enraged heart.

"You won't be on the news. I told them no pictures. They wouldn't dare."

That did it. I would not let this intrusion into her privacy go.

After Bethany was snug in her bed taking a rest, I closed her door — and went into attack mode.

I called her oncologist's office and asked for his nurse. "Does the doctor know about this woman visiting the chemo patients? No one asked our permission! Bethany was in tears!"

The nurse was shocked and knew nothing about the visit. "Let me ask him." Putting me on hold for a moment, she then put him on the line almost immediately.

The doctor, who happened to be on the leadership team of the cancer center, had not been informed about the celebrity visit. He was not happy. He suggested sending a letter to the CEO of the hospital.

I sat down and did just that, expressing my anger in words. "You used us to promote your hospital, and I am outraged. My daughter came home in tears. How could you do that at the worst moment in her life?"

I signed the letter and mailed it as soon as I could.

Within a couple of days, a woman high up in hospital administration visited me in the radiation suite where Bethany was receiving her daily dose of cancer-fighting beams. The anxious visitor pulled me aside.

"How can we make this up to you? We regret this and have informed the young woman of your response."

I looked at her and tried to smile as I weighed my answer. I came up with nothing.

"You can't make this up to us. It's already been done — you can't change what happened."

I accepted her apology but did not have a solution to make her feel better. What was done was done.

I'm certain the young celebrity had no idea how her well-intentioned visit could be perceived as a problem. After all, she just wanted to be kind. But kindness can be misguided, especially when your handlers are looking for promotional opportunities.

The hospital should have known better. They never even asked our permission. After my letter, it was quite clear they understood.

But I was the one left to pick up the pieces of Bethany's hurt. Only God knew the deep grief it caused us both.

Note to self: "Therefore, God's chosen ones, holy and loved, put on heartfelt compassion, kindness, humility, gentleness, and patience, accepting one another and forgiving one another if anyone has a complaint against another. Just as the Lord has forgiven you, so also you must forgive." — Colossians 3:12-13 Forgiveness is not an option, even if a complaint is legitimate. The reality is, in the grip of grief, anger can smother the Holy Spirit. While it's perfectly acceptable to object to an injustice, it is still important to recognize that still small voice prompting forgiveness — whether you feel like forgiving or not.

Note to others: Always ask ahead. Never assume your good intentions will be well received. You may not understand the whole picture.

8

"Nate hit the nail on the head when he said, 'These living years
go by as if they were a puff of smoke in the context of eternity,
but these are the years that really count. We're going to have all
eternity to wish we had done better or feel good about what we
did.' I want so much to make these years count."

— *Bethany's Diary, November 27, 1995*

I t was March and the boys were both home. But we all
knew it would be the last visit with all of us together for
quite some time as Ben was preparing to leave for OCS in Florida.

Dear friends gave him a going away party complete with navy dé-
cor. Nate had come home for the weekend so we could all be together.

I tried to keep a smile on my face, but my heart was breaking.
While I had accepted that it was God's will for my older son to join
the military, my mother's heart was not in sync with my head. I was
hurting not just for me but for Bethany. I knew deep down she would
miss his love and support, and I ached for her loss as well as mine.

March 7 was the big day. Ben left for the navy while we continued our battle against cancer here at home. We had more doctors' appointments that day, while Ben kept his appointment with
Uncle Sam. We prayed that the weapons fighting for Bethany's victory would be as effective as our country's military arms were in
defending the nation.

Although each radiation treatment was short in duration, the six weeks of five-days-a-week appointments were long and arduous. I had attended an evening meeting sponsored by the American Cancer Society that month. What I had surmised during Bethany's treatments was verified by the radiation oncologist who spoke that night. Treatments to the brain completely drain a patient's energy.

Day after day I performed like a cheerleader, coaxing my daughter off the sofa to get up and get in the car. Even when she had mono in high school, I'd never seen her this exhausted. There were times I didn't think I would succeed. Other times I wanted to give up myself because I felt so sorry for her.

But to Bethany's credit, she struggled to get up, get on her coat and will herself to attend one more session. Every day, five days a week, for six weeks. *Bravo, Bethany.*

Her next scheduled round of chemotherapy was to take place a few weeks after the first one. It turned out to be her last. Her blood work afterwards was alarming and her health seriously compromised. One day after a nap, I found her in a sweat.

"Bethany, let's change your shirt, hon." After I helped get her soaked T-shirt over her head, I nearly gasped. Her stomach was covered with petechiae, small broken blood vessels. My nursing knowledge knew her platelets — cells that enabled a person to do normal blood clotting — had to be terribly compromised.

A call to the doctor quickly led to another session at the hospital where Bethany received platelets through an IV.

She was not tolerating these treatments well, at all. While some individuals seem to tolerate chemotherapy, the strong doses of multiple chemicals necessary to destroy her brain cancer seemed intent upon killing my daughter. Some progress has been made in the last ten years with brain cancer treatments. But at that time, there were not as many options.

After discussion with the oncologist, we all agreed. The chemo would stop. Our family prayed that the amount she had already endured was sufficient. None of us wanted the poisonous chemical to continue to attack Bethany. She was under attack enough as it was.

Finally on March 22, the long awaited final radiation treatment was finished. We had planned a celebration that night with her friend Sarah as dinner guest. We all knew how difficult these last weeks had been, and we wanted to cheer Bethany's accomplishment.

But after fixing her a special meal, she slowly rose from her chair and went into the bathroom. I could hear her vomiting.

Sarah and I hurried to help. Bethany had such a strange look on her face. "I made a mess in your sink, Mom."

"That's okay, Bethany. Don't worry about it."

I wasn't worried about the mess. I was concerned about the cause of the vomiting. Radiation can cause swelling in the brain, which, in turn, can cause one to throw up. Bless Sarah's heart, she helped Bethany clean up while I hurried to call the doctor. They told us to bring her to oncology immediately — they would admit her to the hospital.

I was so grateful Sarah was a nursing student. Her training helped her cope without making a fuss. Her friendship throughout Bethany's illness was a gift I will always treasure.

But Bethany's sudden setback was discouraging.

So much for our celebration.

Bethany spent the weekend in the hospital. She was put back on steroids to help with radiation side effects.

It was at this time that I requested a hospital social worker visit us about a power of attorney for medical care. While Bethany was still able to understand and sign her name, we needed to get the proper legal documents in order. Were she ever in a position not to be able to make medical decisions, Steve and I needed to be allowed to do that for her. When a patient is eighteen or older, this is a necessary step. It is just one of many forms that need to be signed when someone has a serious illness.

Amazingly, despite chemo and radiation treatments, Bethany did not lose all of her hair. While every morning would find large clumps on her pillow, she never went completely bald. We had already had her shoulder length hair cut shorter so the falling out wouldn't be as traumatic. But her gift, despite the effects of treatments, was to keep most of her hair. The hats I purchased never needed to be worn. Even patchy hair was a bonus that we treasured, in a world filled with so many difficulties.

We looked for the treasures wherever we could find them.

Note to self: "Every generous act and every perfect gift is from above, coming down from the Father of lights." — James 1:17

Note to others: It is difficult to be around the ill at their worst moments. Pray ahead of time that you will be strong and be an encourager. Not every friend is a nurse, but every friend can remain faithful and be strong with the Lord's help.

9

"Isn't it ironic when you feel so alone in a crowd of people?"

— *Bethany's Diary, September 3, 1996*

There is no loneliness like being a cancer patient.

You may be surrounded by dozens of fellow sufferers in the oncology waiting room with barely an empty chair to find, yet your journey is your own.

Friends may rally around for a time. But they soon go back to their normal lives while patients endure painful blood draws, injections, treatments that make them ill, and separation from those who are healthy.

And while all cancer is horrible, brain cancer often changes the person. In Bethany's case, she was no longer the witty, intelligent, humorous pal her friends had been accustomed to. Her brain damage had robbed her of her former personality. She was a new Bethany, and for those who loved her, it was difficult to witness.

She was also changing physically. She had difficulty speaking and forming her words. Her tone of voice was somewhat flat. Her face was becoming round and her appearance overall was drastically different as she began to put on some weight. Even her walking pattern was stiff and awkward.

It was understandable that many of her friends could not deal with the changes. Some tried to keep in touch. A few even traveled long distances to visit her and bring encouragement. Most, however, dropped out along the way. And as her mom, I wept for this precious loss of companionship at a time when she needed it the most.

Steve reminded me of a day when a previous good friend had said she would come by for a visit. But the friend never showed up. I think I have tried to block some of these memories as much as possible for my own survival. I do not wish to harbor bitterness, nor would a lack of forgiveness serve to hurt anyone except me.

Instead, I focus on the friends and loved ones who were faithful. Family members on the East Coast who rallied around and gave a fundraiser party to help out with her expenses; other family members from California who came out to visit and give her hugs of encouragement; friends from church who sent cards or food or loved on us all in so many ways; other friends whose visits and smiles would light up Bethany's dreary days.

And then there was Sarah. Words cannot express my gratitude to this sweet Christian friend who was faithful to the end.

Sarah was completely accepting of the new Bethany, changes and all. When she was available, Sarah would stay with Bethany on the occasional days when I was asked to substitute for a school nurse who was ill. Sarah often came to have lunch with Bethany or spend an evening watching reruns of *7th Heaven* together. She was the friend who loved unconditionally.

This young lady didn't have to stick with Bethany. Sarah had lots going on in her own life with nursing school and her other friends from church. But she never let us down. She never let Bethany down — and that was who mattered.

Bethany's illness drew her brother Nate home from his internship in St. Louis at least once a month. He was a bundle of humor and lit Bethany's life with joy.

But I knew how awful this change in our lives was for Nate. He was only twenty years old when all this occurred — just starting out on his own — when his lifelong best friend became terminally ill. He and Bethany had been chums since they were tiny, always being silly and sharing a ridiculous sense of humor. Bethany was part mom figure and part co-conspirator in kid crime with her little brother. This impending loss of Nate's sister-buddy was devastating to him.

Yet Nate faithfully came home, either driving the six hours or hopping a quick flight. His presence was a highlight for his sister, and we all appreciated his humor and comfort. We also knew that we could trust him with Bethany if we had to run an errand. He could even stay with her so Steve and I could occasionally go to church together.

Church had become an every other week event for Steve or I, as Bethany was so exhausted and weak from treatments she often could not make it. One of us always had to stay with her.

While I missed going to church regularly, it was also overwhelming when I did get to go. Several friends would swarm around me in comfort and want to know how Bethany was. They were so sweet in their concern. But sometimes talking about it at church left me in tears. There were times I didn't know if it was more difficult emotionally to go to church or stay home.

Steve and I were thrust into a new role with our church friends. We were now the parents of the daughter with a brain tumor. It was an unwelcome role and not a comfortable one. Friends were wonderful, caring and kind. Yet we felt so alone. There is no loneliness like having a dying child. No amount of hugs could change it.

But, paradoxically, their prayers helped us survive it.

Note to self: "Blessed be the God and Father of our Lord Jesus Christ, the Father of mercies and the God of all comfort. He comforts us in all our affliction, so that we may be able to comfort those who are in any kind of affliction, through the comfort we ourselves receive from God." — 2 Corinthians 1:3-4

Note to others: "But the LORD said to Samuel, 'Do not look at his appearance or his stature, because I have rejected him. Man does not see what the LORD sees, for man sees what is visible, but the LORD sees the heart." — 1 Samuel 16:7

Cancer may change the way a person looks. But pray that you can look at them through God's eyes and see the patient the way Jesus would.

Occasionally in life, I will hear someone express the sentiment that, "mercy is not my gift." I tend to disagree with that assumption. I think the gift of mercy is one that everyone can pray for. There will be times that we all will be in need of mercy. It would behoove us all, whether it is our natural inclination or not, to develop empathy for mankind in their most desperate of circumstances. Someday, the desperate one may be staring back at us in the mirror.

10

"Somehow when I'm meeting the needs of others, within His will, my needs get met. Praise God."

— *Bethany's Diary, August 25, 1996*

Steve and I never talked about it, but Ben's upcoming graduation from OCS loomed like the proverbial elephant in the room. We both longed to go, but knew one of us had to stay home. Bethany could never tolerate the trip to Florida and there was no one that we could entrust her with for several days of care. So we avoided the topic for as long as possible.

Then one day in early May, Steve spoke about the elephant.

"I think you should go to Ben's graduation."

I was speechless. After finding my voice, I blurted out, "Are you serious?"

"Yes. I think you need to go."

Throwing my arms around him, I hugged him with relief and joy.

After months of being Bethany's fulltime caregiver, this was the most precious gift I could be offered by the only person who could give it to me. Words could not describe my gratitude.

In an interview years later, I was asked what was the most precious gift my husband had ever given me. Without hesitation I answered, "When my husband sent me to Florida for my son's graduation."

I knew how much he wanted to go. His sacrifice will always be my greatest treasure.

So after making arrangements for a nurse-friend to help with Bethany's hygiene needs while I would be gone, I booked my travel itinerary and planned my personal respite. I was now free to see the culmination of Ben's long weeks of training to become a navy officer.

It was only seven thirty in the morning on that June day, but the heat felt like the tropics at noon. I was in Pensacola, Florida, for Ben's outdoor graduation ceremony. Fanning my face with a program leaflet, I watched my older son parade with the other new officers around the grounds at the Naval Air Station.

My emotions were a blend of pride for Ben, gratitude for Steve, and sadness that we were not all there together. Nate sat beside me, representing our family's support, and we watched in utter fascination at the remarkable transformation that weeks of officer's training had wrought in Ben. Standing tall in his crisp dress uniform, he was now a disciplined military officer, ready to serve his country.

We then were moved into the chapel nearby for the official ceremony. The installation as naval officers was brief but meaningful and the playing of the song "I'm Proud To Be an American" wrung tears from my already fragile emotions. It was an unforgettable moment.

I stood by Ben's side as we were photographed by the official military photographer. I beamed with pride as I squeezed his arm. I knew these strenuous weeks of training had not been easy for him for a multitude of reasons. His commanding military presence did not keep me from seeing the mixed emotions in his heart.

As soon as we were outside, I called Steve to tell him his son was a newly commissioned naval officer. I could hear the pride in his voice, and the sadness that he could not be there to share in the joy. Steve had given Bethany a special pin I had left for her to wear that day in honor of her brother's accomplishment. They were both so excited for him.

All too soon, the weekend was over, the rental car returned, and Nate and I dispersed back to the Midwest, he to St. Louis and I to Des Moines. Ben stayed behind and made arrangements to move into a house with several other officers. He would be coming home soon for a short visit, but then returning to Pensacola to enter flight school. He was officially headed for his upcoming role as a naval flight officer.

I was once again back in my role as fulltime caregiver. But there were no ceremonies to mark the commission — just a commitment to see my daughter through this war on cancer.

It was a battle we prayed would be won. As a nurse, I understood the long term prognosis. And I knew deep down that, shy of a miracle, this would be a war bravely fought, yet inevitably lost.

But our family and friends kept their hope alive each day. So I kept silent about what the future likely held, refusing to shatter everyone's dream.

The nightmare of understanding, however, lay hidden in solitude in my shattered heart.

Note to self: "This is what the LORD says: 'Do not be afraid or discouraged because of this vast multitude, for the battle is not yours, but God's." — 2 Chronicles 20:15

Note to others: Steve's sacrifice for me was the greatest gift as he considered my needs above his own. "Do nothing out of rivalry or conceit, but in humility consider others as more important than yourselves. Everyone should look out not only for his own interests, but also for the interests of others." — Philippians 2:3-4

11

"There is always another battle waiting around the corner. Only when this life in the flesh is over will we be able to rest in the Father's loving, peaceful, conflict-free, perfect, tearless, timeless, glorious presence. When we hear, 'Well done,' it will be over, but no sooner. Until then, the Father allows these light and momentary struggles into our lives (2 Corinthians 4:17) so that He might change us into more useful instruments of righteousness who exist to bring Him the glory He deserves."

— Bethany's Diary, August 26, 1996

Sometimes events throw us into turmoil at the most unexpected times. Such was the case that summer of 2002 when my elderly mom moved from California to Iowa. It had always been my hope that Mom would move to Iowa where Steve and I could watch out for her needs as she aged. We had even purchased a home a few years before that had a bedroom and bathroom on the first floor in anticipation of Mom's future, changing situation. Now she was finally coming but, at the moment, Bethany resided in that very room. And while Mom was not yet in need of fulltime care, I knew she would still be requiring other help if she moved into her apartment in the retirement center a couple of miles away.

I knew she was anxious to be closer to Bethany, and my daughter was thrilled her grandma was going to be within visiting distance. But my feelings were definitely mixed.

I had heard from family members that Mom had fallen occasionally. She refused to use assistive devices such as a cane or walker because she felt they made her look old. I rolled my eyes at such statements, since she was already in her eighties.

But I graciously welcomed her to Iowa, sending her photos of the beautiful new apartment in which she would reside. Looking at those photos that included pictures of Bethany modeling in the mode of a game show hostess, I am saddened by the obvious impact the cancer had imprinted on her. She had little facial expression and her movements were obviously stilted even in still pictures.

So we welcomed Grandma to Iowa as I prayed again for the Lord's strength in an already stressful situation.

Mom had not been in Iowa more than a few weeks when I received a call from her.

"I don't know what happened. I fell and cut my lip. I think I need to go to the hospital."

I inhaled deeply and mustered my patience. "Bethany and I will be right there."

I gathered my slow-moving daughter along with an icepack for Mom, and helped Bethany into the back seat of my car. I had to strap Bethany's seat belt for her as her hands were too weak — a side effect of the tumor's location.

Driving to the beautiful retirement facility, I wondered what shape Mom would be in. The minute I saw her, I knew I would be taking her to the emergency room. I handed her the ice pack to put on her lips and nose, which was swollen as well.

I carefully walked Mom to my car and helped get her seated into the passenger side, assisting her with the seat belt.

Walking around to the driver side, I looked at my little Subaru in a whole new light. My vehicle had transformed into transportation for the handicapped. I had to grin at the thought, before I would groan.

Lord, give me the strength and patience I need.

Driving to the hospital with my two patients, my mom — always concerned about others — twisted as far around in her seat as she could to talk with her granddaughter.

"Bethany, how are you doing?"

My daughter's humor was still intact. I imagined her eyebrows lifting up in surprise as I heard her voice from the back seat.

"Grandma! I'm not the one with an icepack on my face!"

Both Mom and I burst out laughing. Bethany had pointed out the obvious. At the moment, she was doing better than her grandma.

We arrived at the emergency room and I helped both of my patients out of my car. We walked in slow motion into the waiting area where I got both ladies seated while I checked my mom in at the desk. I'm not sure how long we waited in that area, but the entire visit to the ER was at least a couple of hours. Bethany slumped in her chair waiting patiently, but she was so fatigued.

The diagnosis finally came back: Mom not only had cut her lip, requiring stitches by a plastic surgeon, but she had broken her nose.

I began to envision regular visits to the ER.

Before panic would set in, I spoke up to the doctor. "Mom has fallen occasionally and she doesn't remember why she fell today. Could she be evaluated for a walker or cane or something to make her more stable?"

Mom did not look happy at the suggestion, but I would not be deterred. The doctor agreed and set Mom up for an appointment with physical therapy for an evaluation. The physician also arranged for a referral to the specialist who could repair Mom's lip. Nothing could be done for her nose except ice — and the healing of time.

We were all exhausted after our hospital adventure, and I left the patients in the waiting area while I went to get my car.

After driving them to my house, we all collapsed in fatigue.

The appointment with the plastic surgeon was the next day and again, I took both ladies with me for the repair of Mom's lip. Bethany stayed in the waiting area while I stood by Mom's side. I spoke privately with someone at the desk, informing her of my daughter's condition in case she became confused or agitated. The receptionist was understanding and reassuring.

The big appointment with physical therapy was in a few days. When we got there, we discovered a large area filled with tools of the trade — devices to assist those recovering from injury, surgery, or stroke. All the therapists dressed like they were in exercise mode, their tennis shoes adding bounce to their swift strides. They acted as coaches to patients in rehabilitation.

A smiling therapist approached Mom and began asking her questions about her recent fall and other information that would add to her assessment.

The woman was gentle, thorough, and kind. After checking Mom's gait and balance, she determined there were two reasons Mom was falling — an issue with her ankle and with her inner ear.

Then the woman gently suggested that a walker might be something Mom could consider using but, of course, Mom could be the one to decide if she wanted to pursue this.

At this point, I was holding back my frustration but, with measured tongue, pointed out the obvious to the therapist.

"I have a daughter with a brain tumor who is disabled. I need for my mom to have something to keep her from falling. I cannot rescue my Mom every time she falls and then drag my ill daughter around to the emergency room whenever that happens. I need for my mom to use a walker."

There was a slight pause and then my mom spoke. "I never thought of it that way. And you're right."

Much to Mom's credit, she never balked at the idea again. And she was grateful I had spoken up and painted the picture clearly. She now looked at a walker as a helpful solution, not a problem. It was a way she could help the situation. I'll always be grateful she put her wishes aside to see the bigger picture.

Note to self: "Speaking the truth in love, let us grow in every way into Him who is the head — Christ. From Him the whole body, fitted and knit together by every supporting ligament, promotes the growth of the body for building up itself in love by the proper working of each individual part." — Ephesians 4:15-16

Note to others: Keep your eyes and ears open to the needs of caregivers. Sometimes they will speak the words but often will not. Observe a situation and pray for wisdom to know in what ways you can help. Even small decisions like offering to visit a patient and read to them can provide a break for the weary person who watches over them 24-7. It can make all the difference.

"The hearing ear and the seeing eye — the LORD made them both." Proverbs 20:12

12

"*My mind is so jumbled that even my prayers are vague.*"

— *Bethany's Diary, October 18, 1995*

*N*othing went well that morning. And nothing that I did seemed to be right, as far as Bethany was concerned.

I didn't answer her when she called me from the bed to help her get up. I explained I had the water running in the kitchen and I couldn't hear her. She looked at me as if I was making up some lame excuse.

I placed her medications in a bowl next to her breakfast. There were too many pills to take. I explained it was the same number she always took. The oatmeal was terrible. I tried to fix it different-ly. It was still wrong. The juice was wrong. Everything was wrong.

Then it happened.

"I can't do anything right for you!" I screamed, tears running down my face.

Bethany started crying angry tears.

Steve ran into the kitchen, his half-shaved face looking stunned. "What's going on?"

"I can't stand it!" I was out of my mind with exhaustion, fear, and frustration. Bethany didn't understand half of what I'd been doing for her — showering and shampooing her daily, tending to her checkbook to pay her bills, arranging multiple appointments, handling doctors and clinics, the list was endless — and I was losing my ability to cope.

"I can't do anything right." My emotions and body crumpled. Steve took over getting Bethany's breakfast while I left the room to recover.

They call it caregiver stress. Unless you have been there, it's difficult to comprehend the intensity of pain that darkens each and every day. And when you're tending a dying loved one, the anguish is multiplied. Compound the strain with tending to a dying child, and you can reach the breaking point.

I was definitely at that breaking point.

I'm not proud of my outburst that day but I share this scene to let readers know it can happen to any caregiver who is overworked and overstressed. And it was at that point I knew I needed to get more help. If I was to survive this and be the capable nurse for my daughter I needed to be, I had to get more breaks from this schedule — but it would take some planning, as well as trusting others to help. I was fully aware that some who had offered to help were not up to the task for a variety of reasons. Either they expected Bethany to be her old self or they were not sensitive enough to her mental state to be good caregivers.

But prayer brought the right help in many forms.

First, I desperately needed a weekend away. I made plans to visit Ben for a weekend in Florida. He and his navy buddies shared a big house, and Ben said I could sleep in his room. By going away on a weekend, Steve could be Bethany's caregiver and my nurse-friend, Laura, could help my daughter with her personal needs.

In Florida, I met several of Ben's friends, went to his church, and, generally, gave my mind and body a much needed vacation. Occasionally, my heart could not vacation from the pain when others asked how Bethany was, but that was all right. There were moments when the tears needed to let go. But most of the moments were refreshing and rejuvenating to my soul.

After I returned to Iowa, I began making plans to do more substitute nursing at the schools. I needed some normalcy in my life, not to mention the income. I knew that the number of days I could substitute were limited, but even a couple of days a month would be a break.

In August alone that year, Bethany had at least nine different medical appointments including the oncologist, neurologist, and physical therapist. I also was responsible for getting her to social engagements as she could neither drive nor function by herself in any setting. She basically had become like a young child — awkward, unsure of her surroundings, and immature in her decisions. She had gone from independence a year before to complete dependence.

I needed help.

Sarah was going back to school so the hours she could help were limited during the week. There were a couple of friends from church I could trust, and they were a tremendous help, but their availability was limited as well.

I was getting desperate. Then God answered our prayers in the form of a short and stout case manager named Cathy. Her face lit up when she grinned and her bubbly voice filled our living room with hope and encouragement. She was a true godsend.

Cathy was assigned to help Bethany through a program for Iowans with brain damage. She began to navigate the system of caregiving options to help us find suitable assistance. Occasionally the connections were satisfactory. But often the options were limited and did not match my school nurse schedule. We stumbled along as best we could, until one day Cathy suggested an idea that I had not expected — an adult day care center in another town that could watch Bethany during the day twice a week.

At first I balked at the idea.

Leave Bethany in adult day care? I rarely left her in day care as a child. How could I trust my daughter in such a situation? What if someone bothered her? What if she got scared? What if…

My questions were endless and filled with worry.

Cathy understood my concerns and addressed them all. She suggested Steve, Bethany, and I check out the facility that was a thirty-minute drive north. She arranged for us to meet a woman named Jeanne.

Jeanne was a compassionate middle-aged woman with dark hair who had a ready smile and a tragic story of her own. Her brother had suffered permanent brain damage years before, and her passion in life had been to start a facility that would be a place of care and friendship for patients with brain injuries. Most of the clients there had suffered various traumas to the head. Bethany would be the only person there with brain damage from cancer.

Bethany was enthusiastic about the center. I was much more hesitant, inspecting each and every aspect of the staff and the program.

I was impressed that Jeanne spoke directly with Bethany. It's always important to have others speak to the patient, not around them. Despite the brain damage, Bethany could still respond and wanted to participate in discussions.

Bethany was especially upbeat when we visited the adult day care that November afternoon. An MRI the previous month showed she was much better and the cancer was at bay. She thought it was gone completely and informed Jeanne that it was in remission. I did not burst Bethany's bubble of hope, but later, told Jeanne that while the tumor was stopped, it would likely come back.

Since Bethany was so enthused about going to this center, we agreed to try it. I was in tears at the thought, terrified for her safety and well-being.

But my concerns were all laid to rest as Bethany developed friendships there that would make a difference, not just in her life, but in the lives of others.

And ultimately, by trusting God to watch out for Bethany at the adult day center, Steve and I later saw God do a miracle in someone else — long after Bethany had entered eternity.

Note to self: "Let me experience Your faithful love in the morning, for I trust in You. Reveal to me the way I should go, because I long for You." — Psalm 143:8

Note to others: When dealing with a patient who has an illness, try to include them in the conversation. Never talk around them but engage with them. If the topic you bring up seems to be one they do not want to discuss, change the subject to something else. If they seem too tired, limit your visit. But never leave them out of the visit.

"I'm really not worried. I have so much time left to do what He's got planned for me."

—Bethany's Diary, October 10, 1995

It was December 2002, and nearly a year had passed since Bethany's diagnosis. It was also the month of Bethany's twenty-fourth birthday, and she was excited, to put it mildly. Convinced she was cancer-free, she prepared to celebrate her birthday in a big way. I would never dampen her hopes or dreams and encouraged her to rejoice in this awesome occasion. With everything I knew about her particular form of brain cancer, it would likely return at some point and with a vengeance. But I would enjoy this celebration of her life and ignore what my mind was telling me: This would likely be her last birthday.

It took her time and patience to create a flyer, but Bethany managed to write all the words, inviting friends and family to participate in what she entitled her "Celebrate Life" party. She wrote… *"I am emerging as an even better Bethany, ready and happy to celebrate two dozen years this December 12, the life I didn't lose, and the coming holiday season."*

She seemed to feel like a butterfly emerging from a cocoon of cancer.

When I think of all the trauma her brain had endured at this point, it seems like a miracle she was able to create such beautiful wording for the invitation.

Music filled the house as friends from church and family members gathered to share in her birthday joy, swarming around her with love and words of encouragement. Laughter echoed in the rooms and refreshments were enjoyed as we all rejoiced that Bethany was stable, happy, and, although a changed person, still the same sweet spirit we had always loved.

But I inwardly cringed every time I heard her declaring to a party guest she was healed of her cancer. I didn't recall any doctor telling her that. It was her interpretation of the MRI's that said the cancer did not appear to be growing. She grasped on to that hope by declaring she was cancer free.

If only that were so.

Details of this last birthday party are so sketchy in my memory. I recall feeling like I was two people: I was Bethany's mom who was smiling and happy to celebrate the day. But the other mom — the nurse-mom — simmered with fear and trepidation about what lay ahead.

How long will this evil tumor stay at bay? How many more birthdays, if any, will be shared with my daughter? How long will everyone believe my daughter is actually healed and on the road to recovery? How long can I keep up this façade of happily ever after?

The struggle was waged throughout the evening as my inner battle was shielded from view by my smiling face.

Looking back, there were probably others there who shared my fears. And looking back, I realize that December held the last of our happy days together. The darker days ahead would, all too soon, envelop us once again.

Note to self: "You don't even know what tomorrow will bring — what your life will be! For you are a bit of smoke that appears for a little while, then vanishes." — James 4:14

Note to others: "For My thoughts are not your thoughts, and your ways are not My ways.' This is the LORD's declaration. 'For as heaven is higher than earth, so My ways are higher than your ways and My thoughts than your thoughts." — Isaiah 55:8-9

"I used to pray that God would make me stronger, but now I ask Him to make me weaker. That way His power can manifest all the more."

— *Bethany's Diary, October 9, 1995*

Her eyes stared at me with a darkness I had come to fear. "You put something in my juice." Her flat tone of voice heightened with a certainty in her paranoia that sent chills of remembrance through me. And with her decisive accusation and alien gaze, I recalled her accusations of the previous January and was certain of the terrible truth. The tumor was back and spreading.

Dear Lord, help us.

I struggled to swallow. "Bethany, I didn't put anything in your glass other than juice. All of your medicines are in the bowl. They're the same ones you've been taking for a long time."

Her black gaze continued. "You put something in my drink. I know you did." Her eyes narrowed with distrust.

"You don't have to drink it if you don't want. But I didn't put anything in your glass other than juice."

Taking the cup from her, I trembled at the realization of what might be happening. A few days after her birthday the previous month, her headaches had increased. They were so severe the doctor started her on a narcotic pain patch. Once again, she imagined others were harming her or plotting against her. Were tumor cells growing? I feared the worst.

I called the doctor, and they ordered an MRI. He also upped the dose of one of her behavior meds to prevent a repeat of the previous January events. I called Steve and tried to keep the tone in my voice level. Panic would not help either of us.

We were scheduled to drive downtown that day to pick up concert tickets at the box office for the Des Moines Symphony. I worried this change in her behavior might make even that simple journey impossible. Somehow we managed to achieve that errand without any further dramatic events ensuing.

The tickets to the symphony were part of Bethany's Christmas present from a couple of weeks earlier. We had purchased an extra so she could take a friend of her choice. She decided to invite Steven, a young man whom she had met at the adult day care center she attended twice a week. Steven had brain damage and was blind from a car accident he had been in a few years before.

He was a regular at the care center and, as two of the younger participants in the daycare, Bethany and he became close friends. One weekend we took Steven to a movie with Bethany, then stopped for a bite to eat. It was a wonderful friendship for her in her isolated state, especially because most of her friends from a year earlier were too busy to visit her anymore.

Bethany spoke with Steven about God and His Son Jesus Christ on more than one occasion. But Steven wanted nothing to do with God or faith. His reality was in the here and now.

In the meantime, the here and now for Bethany included that MRI to determine if the tumor was indeed spreading. Bethany had already been through numerous scans of her brain. For the first few, she managed with minimal stress the isolation in the large MRI tube with its jack-hammer-like noise. But as time went on, she became more and more claustrophobic, necessitating someone to be in there with her. It was usually me.

I'd bring along some soothing music that she could listen to in the headphones. I rubbed her feet to keep her calm. I spoke softly to her in between the irritating sounds of the machine. And I'd pray — pray the scan would be over soon and if there was anything we needed to know, the images would reveal it.

The MRI was finished and the scans sent to the doctor. The diagnosis from the radiologist stated there were no changes from the previous MRI. Both the neurologist and the oncologist agreed — the scans looked the same.

I knew in my heart they were wrong. But I prayed that I was.

It was at that point that I began to distrust the diagnostic ability of man's machinery. It is as prone to error as people are.

Note to self: While distrusting what the doctors were saying, I had to pray for wisdom and discernment and realize if I was right and the tumor had returned, time would reveal the situation. "It is better to take refuge in the LORD than to trust in man." — Psalm 118:8

Note to others: Understand our wisdom and medical knowledge is limited. While we would like to think doctors diagnose properly every time, they are imperfect in their humanity. They would be the first to admit it.

"And so I thank the Lord for my weakness and inability to handle past, present, and future problems. When I am weak, that is when He is strong."

— *From Bethany's Diary (No date given)*

One of Bethany's doctors listened to our concerns about Bethany's increasing symptoms and sent us back to the neuropsychologist.

We had visited this specialist the previous October, and he had given Bethany a series of tests to determine what impact the tumor had made on her psychological processes and behaviors.

With her recent behavioral changes but lack of diagnostic verification from the MRI, the doctors wondered if anything further could be assessed through this doctor's testing.

The neuropsychologist was a friendly man, kind, and probably just a few years older than Bethany. He always listened carefully to our concerns — always the mark of a good healthcare provider — and took notes. After he considered what Bethany and I told him, he stood up and escorted her to the testing room where she would answer questions, most of which involved using pen and paper. Some were verbal tests.

It was a lengthy test — over an hour — and as usual, I brought my crocheting. I could not count the number of hours I'd spent in waiting rooms over the last year, but those minutes added up as I completed more than one large afghan during that time.

Moments in the waiting room were also a time when I would have brief connections with other family members of patients. There's always a community of injured hearts in hospital waiting areas. They can prompt you to be more compassionate towards other's needs and get your mind off of your own concerns and fears. At least for a few moments.

Waiting for the neuropsychologist on this particular day, I was surprised when they both appeared in a shorter time than expected. I focused on his sober face. He was holding the papers and looking troubled. Inviting us both into his office, we all sat down.

I do not recall his exact words, but I remember his concern. He said it had not gone well and she had dropped in her test scores dramatically. Perhaps we needed to retest at a later time. Perhaps she was tired today.

It seemed to me that he was greatly concerned but was hoping against hope that he was wrong. I knew in my heart he was not.

I also understood that this neuropsychologist, like so many others in the medical world as well as the lay community, could not come to grips with the changes that were occurring in this formerly brilliant young woman, now rendered brain damaged. And it appeared she was getting worse.

As Bethany's mom, I was forced to come to grips with the situation on a daily basis. And as her mom, without affirmation from others about my deepening fear, I felt like I was living alone on a planet of reality while the rest of the world lived in a land of make-believe.

Was I just giving up hope? Or was I a realist while others lived in a dream world?

One thing was certain — without God to turn to and share my darkest fears, I would have sunk into deep despair.

Note to self: "Casting all your care upon Him, because He cares about you." — 1 Peter 5:7

"The righteous cry out, and the LORD hears, and delivers them from all their troubles. The LORD is near the broken-hearted; He saves those crushed in spirit." — Psalm 34:17-18

Note to others: It is not helpful to dismiss a patient's or caregiver's concerns. Sometimes they need to verbalize their fears and not be told that everything will be fine. While it is wonderful to be encouraging, giving false hope stops open communication. It is far better to listen and pray for wisdom about what to say. Sometimes, if you still don't know what to say, it's all right to admit that. None of us knows the appropriate words to speak all the time. Not even writers.

"Life isn't just some rat race to be run and when you're done, you get some cheese. The cheese is nice, and the points accumulated along the way are good, but there is too much along the way to ignore. Yes, I need to dream and hope and keep working towards that day when I can hear, 'Well done,' but each day (each moment really) is as much a gift as 'the cheese.'"

— Bethany's Diary, September 18, 1995

I noticed the awkward gate of our Welsh corgi, Rosie, as I placed her in her nighttime kennel.

"Are you okay, Rose?" She settled down on her blanket with a thud and appeared prepared to snooze. I was exhausted as usual at the end of a day and thought no further about her wobbly, slow legs.

Checking to make sure the baby monitor was on at Bethany's bedside, I pushed the button to start her *Caedmon's Call* CD and kissed Bethany's soft cheeks.

"Goodnight, sweetie."

"Night, Mama." Bethany nestled under her covers, hugging one of the stuffed animals that inhabited her bedroom.

Struggling up the stairs to our bedroom, my only goal at the moment was getting some sleep. I collapsed into my bed next to Steve, barely remembering the music from the CD coming through the monitor receiver.

The next thing I remember hearing was Bethany's voice from

the monitor in the middle of the night. She was talking about nothing in particular, but the fact she was awake at all was disturbing. Her nighttime meds usually calmed her enough to help her sleep. This chatter was completely unexpected and disturbing.

I pulled myself out from under the covers and awkwardly descended the stairs. Bethany's eyes were wide open and she was speaking about nothing in particular.

"Bethany? What's going on?" I yawned.

"I can't sleep." This sounded alarmingly familiar.

I mentally calculated if she'd taken all of her medications the night before. I hadn't actually watched her ingest them, but she was usually very good about taking them all. Of course, her weak hands sometimes had difficulty…

Then it hit me like a bolt of lightning in the middle of a midnight storm: She must have dropped one of her pills and Rosie ate it!

It was too late now to take Rosie to the vet. Pumping her stomach would not remove the medication she had likely swallowed. It would long since be in her system.

All we could do was wait — and pray.

After a restless night of monitoring Bethany, the sun finally rose and I checked our canine pal. She was very much under the influence of something.

I phoned the vet after I knew his office was open and explained the situation. At first he feared the dog might have eaten chemotherapy. We assured him it wasn't that but, whichever pill it was, she could barely walk. We gave him the list of possible medications. He said all we could do was monitor her and if she got worse, to bring her in.

For two days, Rosie was not herself, stumbling around, and causing us concern. By the third day, however, she burst out of her kennel in the morning, her enthusiastic personality back to its rambunctious norm. Rosie would survive!

We thanked God that, in the midst of all this turmoil and difficulty, our God spared us from losing our beloved pet. It was one more gift on this journey.

Note to self: Focus on the simple joy of an answered prayer. Even though the larger prayer — Bethany's healing — did not seem to be progressing, God sent numerous messages of His love and care for us in such moments as Rosie's recovery.

Note to others: Ask a caregiver for specific prayer requests for the patient as well as the family. An answered prayer may be the only hope they have in an otherwise hopeless situation.

Note to All: Be very careful with medications you keep in the house. Some of them are highly dangerous if taken by children or pets. Keep them up high and locked away. After the incident with Rosie, I monitored Bethany whenever she took her pills to be sure they were all swallowed by her and did not fall onto the floor.

"I want to fall in love someday. I'm ever so curious about it and eager for it, but I know that such things must never be rushed. I would like to look nice for whomever the Lord chooses. I wonder if I will."

— Bethany's Diary, April 26, 1996

The afternoon of the much anticipated symphony finally arrived. Driving to the beautiful Civic Center, we spoke with Steven about his love of music. He was familiar with classical pieces and excited about the program of Russian compositions that were in the lineup. Somehow I imagined he would only like rock music, but Jeanne at the adult day center informed us otherwise.

Walking up the numerous steps was a challenge for Bethany, but she succeeded in the climb, as did Steven using his white cane and holding on to Steve's coat for direction. We settled into our plush seats, surrounded by the hundreds of other attendees finding their assigned chairs.

Bethany and I sat in between the two men, Steven next to her and Steve next to me. The lights lowered and a hush fell over the crowd.

The maestro arrived on stage to immediate applause, and we all shifted in anticipation of the music. It was everything we had hoped it would be: rich, powerful, and inspiring.

Moment after moment of tender refrains followed by crescendos of explosive melodies filled the room with excitement and awe.

But then an even more dramatic scene unfolded next to me — something I had not anticipated — and my already wounded heart was in danger of breaking to pieces.

Bethany had jerked slightly in her seat, and Steven, although blind, had felt the movement.

"Are you all right?" I heard his whisper in between violin strings.

"Yeah." Bethany's voice hushed her reply.

Then it happened. I heard Steven whisper, "Can I hold your hand?" My heart lurched.

"Yes." Her reply rippled with tenderness.

He reached over and gently took her small hand into his as they listened to the orchestra.

And as the resounding melodies pealed through the auditorium, the pain in my heart poured out onto my cheeks. Her hopes and dreams for love and marriage could never be fulfilled.

That realization stabbed into my heart with the pain of a thousand knives. A part of me died that afternoon.

Note to self: "Be gracious to me, LORD, because I am in distress; my eyes are worn out from angry sorrow — my whole being as well. Indeed, my life is consumed with grief, and my years with groaning;" — Psalm 31:9-10

Note to others: Many years ago, I listened to a pastor speaking about grief and about a family in his church who had lost a child. He felt helpless to offer the right words of comfort to the sorrowing parents, and then he realized a great yet simple truth. "Sometimes, all you can do is cry with them."

"Jesus wept." — John 11:35

18

"My Father is in control. I will rejoice and be glad in each day He gives me. You know feelings come and go, but the truth will always be a constant. God will always love me."

— *Bethany's Diary, March 25, 1996*

*M*om was a frequent dinner guest at our house, and Bethany reveled in the extra attention. She especially loved being read to, and Grandma was more than willing to do the honors.

It was a challenge providing entertainment for Bethany that would not confuse or frighten her. Even programs that were harmless in their storyline might have a commercial sponsor that displayed frightening images that could upset her.

Her ability to mentally process her environment was so hampered that we were ever vigilant about stories that were discussed or images displayed around her. It was just like protecting a young child. So reading provided the perfect entertainment — with no commercial intrusions.

One night after dinner, Grandma read to Bethany from one of the James Herriot books. As Steve sat in the family room and I crocheted, we all listened to the amazing true-life adventures of the veterinarian from Yorkshire, England. Most of the stories are amusing or heartwarming, but a few get quite technical about the science of veterinary medicine. The particular chapter my mom read that evening happened to be about artificial insemination in cows.

It started out innocent enough but soon progressed into technical narrative that caused mom to stumble a bit in her reading.

I can still envision my very proper mother with graying hair and reading glasses, reciting the words. As the medical phrases and bovine anatomy were described in startling detail, Mom's discomfort seemed to be increasing. Struggling somewhere between sympathy for my mom and the desire to explode with laughter, I couldn't help but giggle. I noticed Bethany was smiling as well. Steve attempted to keep a straight face but soon lost the battle.

Then Mom plopped the open book on her lap. "Really!" She was exasperated and embarrassed.

We all burst out laughing.

"Do you want me to take over, Mom?"

Taking in a deep breath, Mom laughed. "No, I can finish it." She picked up the hardbound volume again and bravely began to read.

Finally getting through the embarrassing chapter, she set the book down with obvious relief.

We all giggled for weeks after that, every time we remembered the evening of James Herriot and the cows — and the revelation of more veterinary information than we ever wanted to know!

Note to self: In the midst of pain and sorrow, moments of sheer laughter are a balm to the soul. "He will yet fill your mouth with laughter and your lips with a shout of joy." — Job 8:21

Note to others: Sometimes the best gift you can give to patients and caregivers is a diversion. It might be a DVD, a book, or anything that, for a time, can replace difficulty with laughter. Truly good medicine for a broken spirit as it says in Proverbs 17:22.

"Someday I will write a book, and it will be a work of art. Lovingly printed on the inside of the front cover of each copy, it will read, 'Daddy this is for you. I love you.'"

— *Bethany's Diary, June 22, 1995*

Bethany loved her dad. From the time she was little and had graduated off of my lap, she enjoyed spending time with her daddy. As she got older, she loved talking to her father about his work as a writer for a newspaper and then for magazines. She had always hoped to become a writer. Now, it seemed, that plan might be permanently on hold.

Steve and Bethany always shared a love of old movies, so while Bethany was ill, he rented numerous comedies and musicals. Bethany especially loved Esther Williams' movies, where the starlet would do amazing swimming feats. The actress would always perform spectacular numbers surrounded by a bevy of lady swimmers adding to the astonishing routines. Some of the choreography would send Bethany and Steve into belly laughs.

Something had changed this spring of 2003, however. No longer could Bethany focus on a two hour or less movie. She started to fall asleep midway through. Soon she couldn't stay awake more than a few minutes. Soon she didn't want to watch them at all.

Steve says she just could not focus. She seemed fearful and disconnected. Her headaches increased and the doctor slowly increased her narcotic pain patch.

How could this tumor not be back? I was so frustrated that no one would give us answers.

We tried to continue our normal routine. I continued to substitute on occasion at the schools while Bethany stayed at adult day care. But her activity at the day care became less interactive. They had a bed there and she would often nap for long periods. She was far more disconnected there as well.

Hoping to brighten her spirits at the end of March, I took her to the Botanical Gardens. Spring had not yet come to Iowa, but it was always summer at the indoor garden a few miles away. It was a refreshing respite, but she was too tired to walk around very much.

By early April, her cousin, Renee, came for a visit from California. She was so accepting of the changes in Bethany and smothered her with hugs and kisses. She also bought a soft bear for Bethany that became one of her favorite stuffed animals. Shopping excursions were becoming few and far between so this event stands out in my mind as one of the only enjoyable outings we had.

Despite the blooming spring weather, dark clouds of cancer hovered over our world. Summer seemed to be a lifetime away.

The increasing changes in Bethany prompted me to call her doctor once again. I knew this wretched tumor was back, and we needed to come up with a plan. He agreed that something was happening, and he referred us to a specialist at the University of Iowa. Perhaps he could help.

Before our appointment on May 12, I made one last trip to Pensacola for a weekend visit to see Ben and have some rest and relaxation from caregiving and work.

I had a terrible suspicion it would be my last opportunity to get away for quite some time. And I also knew in my heart, I would need the strength for the tumultuous journey that lay ahead.

Note to self: "Come to Me, all of you who are weary and burdened, and I will give you rest. All of you, take up My yoke and learn from Me, because I am gentle and humble in heart, and you will find rest for yourselves." Matthew 11:28-29

Note to others: My son Ben and his fellow officers and friends in Pensacola were so gracious to provide me with respite from the heavy burden at home. I am forever grateful to them for their hospitality, and I made sure to prepare a home-cooked meal for them in thanks. Even though I am not a great chef, they seemed to appreciate it. "Be hospitable to one another without complaining." — 1 Peter 4:9

"It's funny how sometimes life seems unreal. You could be doing a job or talking to a friend or just sitting and all of a sudden it feels like you're not important and they're not important, it's just God. You don't even name it God, you just feel His omnipotence and love. You think, 'Life is so precious. It's here, then it's gone.'"

— *Bethany's Diary, August 16, 1995*

G athering up the multiple MRI images of my daughter's brain, we headed for Iowa City. Steve drove while Bethany sat in the back seat.

It was a gorgeous May morning, and spring had truly come to Iowa with the splendid greenery I cherished. Winter had been too long. Yet even with the sunshine and emerging life around us, I felt the gloom of impending death. I wanted to ignore it, but it hovered over me like storm clouds that threatened a tornado. If the whirlwind hit us, how would we survive? I stared out the window, occasionally adjusting the radio volume. I longed to think of anything else.

The drive took over two hours to reach the University of Iowa Hospitals and Clinics in Iowa City. The campus was large, requiring lots of walking, so we borrowed one of their wheelchairs to shuttle Bethany down the long corridors. Reaching the oncology offices, we were ushered to a waiting area. Another waiting area.

Instead of my crocheting, however, I clutched the stack of MRI images that had so far not revealed anything. Would this doctor see something no one else did?

We were called back after several moments by a smiling young woman. The nurse brought us into the small examination room and asked us questions. When she was finished, a female resident came in. She examined Bethany and asked a thousand questions.

"The doctor will be in shortly." She smiled as she exited, chart in hand.

That's the problem with a teaching hospital: You have to see the doctors-in-training first, then wait for the real doctor. But that's also the blessing of teaching hospitals: They train new doctors to replace the experienced ones.

We waited. And waited. The clock on the wall clicked its presence and I smiled at Bethany.

What is she thinking? She must be terrified. I know I am.

Finally an older doctor with a warm smile entered the room. He shook all of our hands and sat down with us. And then he did something that no doctor before had done.

"Tell me the whole story, from the beginning." He held his pen and took notes, occasionally asking us for clarification. When had this occurred? When did we notice this?

He was the most thorough doctor we had encountered in this whole experience. Not only did he want to see the MRI scans but he wanted to know the sequence of events and everything about the patient, not just the images on the screen. He checked those scans, in between listening. I've never been more grateful to have someone really listen.

He also asked questions of Bethany, and then Steve gave his input.

Finally, when I completed the story, I said the words we all feared. "I'm worried the tumor is growing again."

He finished writing his notes, then looked up. "I think you're right."

I was finally hearing the verification I had known for the last four months. But hearing the words spoken audibly was heart-stopping.

The doctor pointed at the recent images and explained, based on my narrative of events, the path the tumor had taken. The man was brilliant, describing the insidious journey the tentacles of cancer had taken. He even pointed to a murky area on the new scan that showed probable new cancer cells. It was a cloudy area that other professionals had missed.

Steve, Bethany, and I sat in stunned silence, taking in his every word. Bethany said nothing. Steve and I asked a few questions.

The doctor said we should visit Bethany's local oncologist who might have some ideas for other therapies. But if he was right, nothing would help in the long run. He said he would consult with his colleagues to get their opinion before giving a final diagnosis.

We thanked him for his help and evaluation and shook his hand with stiffened fingers. He shook Bethany's limp hand. I can't imagine what was going through his mind. Surely he knew this would be the last time he would see her.

We gathered our things and left the oncology area. It was lunchtime and we all needed some sustenance. Finding a cafeteria, we bought some food and tried to enjoy it. We did not speak about the appointment we had just come from, but finished eating and left.

The drive home was silent.

Bethany eventually fell asleep. When I noticed she'd been asleep for awhile, I breathed in some courage.

"Did the doctor say the tumor was back and growing?" I stared at Steve, hoping he'd tell me I was wrong.

He swallowed visibly. "Yes."

We didn't speak anymore until we got home. After we let the dogs outside, Steve and Bethany sat on the couch. He put his arm around her shoulders and let her cry.

At such a moment, I could not sit and cry. I had to keep moving, clean up, do something — anything — so I wouldn't have to think about the words the doctor had spoken. I knew if I started to cry, I would not stop weeping, and my strength would be sapped. I needed to be strong for Bethany.

I needed all the strength I could muster for this terrifying journey ahead.

Note to self: "Do not fear, for I am with you; do not be afraid, for I am your God. I will strengthen you; I will help you; I will hold on to you with My righteous right hand." — Isaiah 41:10

Note to others: Everyone reacts differently when they are given devastating news. Through the many months of our daughter's cancer, Steve and I took turns being the strong one. When we arrived home after the earthshaking doctor's appointment, Steve was able to be the comforter. I felt so overwhelmed I wanted to run away. I did so by keeping busy. Never assume you know how anyone should react when they are grieving. What you see on the outside does not reflect the state of their heart. My heart at that moment was so overwhelmed with grief, I felt numb — and terrified. The grief strangled my ability to express any emotion at all. I'm certain I must have appeared like a moving statue without a soul. But my petrified soul mourned inconsolably.

21

"My Heavenly Father has so lovingly bestowed upon me the gift of moments. Moments are numerous, yet each one is priceless. How long is a moment? Well, if you blink, it's gone, but if you can hold your gaze, drink in the beauty that surrounds you, a moment can last forever."

— *Bethany's Diary, August 26, 1995*

*S*tanding outside the school where I substituted as school nurse, I drank in the surrounding scene from atop the hill. Everything seemed so peaceful in that quiet neighborhood, but a battle of fear waged in my mind.

It was late May and, while the sun shone and the air was warm, a chill enveloped me.

My thoughts tried to focus on anything except the phone call I'd just received. It was the doctor from Iowa City and his colleagues had confirmed the diagnosis: Bethany's brain tumor was back. In the course of eternity, her moments left with us on earth would be relatively few.

It was news I'd expected, but the reality was beginning to sink in. It hurt, unlike any pain I'd ever experienced before.

Why God? Why has this happened? Was she exposed to a toxic substance at some point? Was she born with the cancer and it lay dormant for years? Was it her cell phone sending damaging radiation into her brain?

These were questions that could not be answered, nor was it ultimately a helpful contemplation. In this life, I would never know. But what I did know was that we needed to come up with a way to help her through these final moments on earth.

I returned to the nurse's office and thanked the secretary for covering for me while I took the expected call. The staff was so kind and caring — their compassion made it difficult to stem the tide of tears. But I had to finish my shift as long as the children needed me. Thank God it was just a half-day.

The appointment with Bethany's local oncologist was that Friday. Steve came with Bethany and me, and we were seated in a small room that felt even smaller when the physician entered, accompanied by a resident student.

Bethany's doctor had read the report from the specialist in Iowa City. He was very businesslike, yet I could see this was painful news for him as well. He had always been very caring and concerned while maintaining a professional attitude. But even well trained physicians are flesh and blood, and they feel a family's loss when all their efforts to heal a patient are unsuccessful.

He discussed what options were possible. There was a new oral chemo that was a trial drug that might help. He could not say if it might make her ill again, as the previous chemotherapy had. He admitted it might make her sick and, in the long run, might not make any difference at all in the amount of time she had left.

I looked at Bethany who sat very still and quiet. Her expression was blank. Did she know what he was saying?

"Bethany? Do you understand what they're saying?" I wanted her to comprehend so she could help decide.

She understood completely, as tears began to roll down her cheeks.

The student doctor turned toward the wall. He looked lost. Had he ever participated in telling a patient they were dying? A patient not much younger than himself? Behind his white jacket, I knew his heart was touched by this moment. I sometimes wonder if he remembers Bethany even today.

❋ ❋ ❋

At home we discussed the pros and cons of trying the new drug. I was opposed, remembering the impact the first chemo had on her already fragile system. Steve thought it might be a good idea. Bethany was conflicted.

How do you decide such an option when either way, she will die? Ultimately, we decided that her time left with us was worth making as pleasant as possible, without the interference of more chemicals with the potential to make her miserable. Perhaps even hasten her death. Since radiation was no longer an option either, we decided to rely on prayer.

Prayer had been my mainstay from the beginning — even before Bethany was diagnosed with this terrible cancer.

Morning quiet time with the Lord had long been a habit. I would read the Bible and a short devotional, and pray. I'm so grateful the Lord had impressed upon me the need for starting each day with Him, years before this crisis. Because it was such a part of my routine, I felt lost without drinking in the Lord's presence each morning, much as I would drink a cup of tea. It was pure sustenance.

After Bethany was diagnosed, there were mornings it was more difficult to make that time with the Lord happen. But I persisted in doing daily devotions as frequently as possible.

During Bethany's illness, our CD player ran most of each day with praise and worship music by Michael W. Smith and other

Christian artists. It set the tone in our home for moment-by-moment dependency on God.

Not long after Bethany's diagnosis, her pastor came to our home, anointed her with oil and prayed for her healing.

And yet here we were, facing her impending death.

Did I feel all of this was for nothing? That God had deserted us or let us down, even when we were trusting in Him?

In John 16:33, Jesus said, "…in Me you may have peace. You will have suffering in this world. Be courageous! I have conquered the world."

Our comfort is not in what this world has to offer. It never offers us eternity. Only Jesus offers that.

Note to self: Jesus said, "Peace I leave with you. My peace I give to you. I do not give to you as the world gives. Your heart must not be troubled or fearful." — John 14: 27

Note to others: Sometimes a patient and family are left with difficult decisions about treatments. Do we take every medication available? Do we choose some treatments but not all? Do we choose alternative treatments? Will insurance cover all the treatments? These decisions are painful and can leave patients and their families uncertain and conflicted.

There are no universal right answers. A patient must listen to all the options and decide. Ultimately there is not a single right answer for everyone; only the right answer for that individual.

"You know I'm not very good at being a Christian. The Lord told me that His strength is perfect, though. 1 Corinthians I believe. Wow, with all of my weaknesses, He must be stronger than I can even fathom."

— *Bethany's Diary, December 1, 1995*

That June, Bethany continued to attend the care center just because she loved it. I didn't need someone else to watch out for her during the summer months when school was out. But she loved the camaraderie of her fellow brain-injured friends, and she always looked forward to seeing them.

The effect of the spreading cancer, however, began to display itself in insidious manifestations, one of which was stress while riding in the car. The thirty-minute trip to the care facility was becoming even more anxiety filled. Strapped next to me in the passenger seat, she shared it was all she could do not to open the door and jump out of the car — en route! Those were not calming words to my ears.

I remember one trip when I talked to her all the way to distract her from carrying out an escape plan while the car was moving. We both breathed a huge sigh of relief when we arrived.

The day came, though, when she was almost too weak to get out to the car in the driveway. It was no more than twenty feet to the Subaru, but to Bethany, it might as well have been twenty miles.

She was anxious to get to the event the care center had planned:

a picnic in the park. I knew she felt so weak that morning, but she insisted she could make it.

Struggling to help her get dressed and ready, we were both exhausted by the time she'd gotten out the door.

When we made it out to the porch, I wondered if she could proceed with her much-desired plan.

Her stiff legs didn't want to move, try as she might. I helped her each step of the way, but by the time she descended the first stair, she sat down with a thud.

Lord, I'm not strong enough. Help me!

"Bethany, are you sure you should go?" A twinge in my back reminded me of the injury I'd sustained years ago when working in the hospital. Also, I have limited strength in one hand. What could I do? But Bethany looked at me with pleading eyes.

"I want to go."

Tears threatened us both as desperation swept over me. I knew this might be her last visit with her friends. The writing was on the wall. How much longer could she and I do this? But she longed to go — just one more time.

Just when I thought there was no hope, I heard a voice approach from behind. Our neighbor!

He was a hard-edged Vietnam veteran who spoke little but smoked a lot. He didn't interact with others much, but he'd obviously seen our dilemma. And his heart responded.

"Do you need some help?"

"Yes!" I wanted to hug him.

His arms lifted Bethany to her feet, and he gently helped her down the three steps to the ground. Our gruff neighbor supported her as she walked to the car. I hurried ahead and opened the car door, while he guided her into the seat. She looked at him with eyes of gratitude and whispered, "Thanks."

After clicking her seat belt, I closed the door and held him with my grateful gaze. "You have no idea how much your help means to us."

He brushed it off. "Glad I could help."

Sauntering back towards his house, I watched the veteran leave as quietly as he'd arrived.

I don't know if he was ever a hero in the war. But on that day, he was a hero to me.

Note to self: Never judge someone by their outward appearance or demeanor. "Now we who are strong have an obligation to bear the weaknesses of those without strength, and not to please ourselves. Each one of us must please his neighbor for his good, in order to build him up." — Romans 15:1-2

Note to others: If anyone thinks they are not good enough to help in God's Kingdom, they might try to see themselves through God's eyes. He is the ultimate equalizer in our worth.

"Carry one another's burdens; in this way you will fulfill the law of Christ. For if anyone considers himself to be something when he is nothing, he is deceiving himself." — Galatians 6:2-3

23

"My only ray of hope is that the Lord will be with me, through the good and the bad. He will help me and love me just the same. Thank God for that promise."

—*Bethany's Diary, January 2, 1996*

That summer we had to face the hardest decision of all — signing Bethany up for hospice care.

The incident on the porch was just one of the deciding factors. Getting anywhere or doing anything was becoming not just difficult, but almost impossible. We called the doctor's office and he took care of the details. Hospice would help Bethany in our home.

While there was a residential facility not far away, sending our daughter to live elsewhere was not an option in our eyes. She needed us now more than ever, and I would never sleep or be at peace leaving her in the complete care of others. We wanted her home.

I had never dealt with hospice before, but I quickly learned the advantages of the program. They provide end-of-life care when the patient is expected to have less than six months to live. All of their care is directed towards keeping the patient comfortable during their last days. No medicines such as chemotherapy are given to attempt to prolong life, but medications to keep a patient comfortable are provided as needed.

When you become a part of the hospice system, a patient is assigned a team of workers. We were blessed to learn that Bethany's primary nurse was a Christian. What a comfort to be able to talk freely with Sandy about Jesus and His work in our lives, even in such a desperate time.

She was a gift in so many ways. Her enthusiastic personality and infectious laugh brightened each day that she came for Bethany's checkups. My daughter loved Sandy and always gave huge grins at her arrival. Sandy even appreciated the presence of our two Welsh corgis, who greeted her like she was a member of the family.

One of Bethany's team members, however, made me very uncomfortable. As a nurse and a mom, I have learned to trust my instincts with people. Nothing ever occurred to cause outright suspicion, but I did not feel I could trust this team member. It was only a short time before I requested a replacement.

It was definitely the right decision, as the replacement was a lovely woman named Dorothy. I will never forget how she would bring the party to Bethany when my daughter couldn't get out and about anymore. Dorothy was a delight and another treasure in this journey. And then there was Roberta. She was a retired nurse who volunteered for hospice. She became a precious friend to all of us in the last months of Bethany's life.

This was the group who helped us on a journey we never wanted to take. Yet their guidance helped us navigate the unfamiliar waters of fear and grief. Without their help and guidance, we might have drowned.

Note to self: "And my God will supply all your needs according to His riches in glory in Christ Jesus." — Philippians 4:19

Note to others: While you may find yourself or a loved one assigned to a health care provider, that does not mean you must keep that worker, physician or whomever. Consider yourself a consumer. If the fit is wrong, ask for another. Sometimes it may be a personality clash or perhaps you are dissatisfied with their care for a number of reasons. You are allowed to speak up.

"As I rest contentedly in the strong, yet gentle arms of the Creator, I look into His eyes. Those eyes see through to the deepest part of me and love me just the same. They are beauty personified and love in its truest form. They are the eyes of my Father, and I will ever remain in their sight."

— *Bethany's Diary, December 12, 1995 (her seventeenth birthday)*

*H*ospice not only sent helpful staff, they provided much needed supplies such as a wheelchair, hospital bed, and shower chair.

I was never more grateful for the wide doorways in our old home. They allowed ample room to wheel Bethany around when she was too tired to walk. But while transporting her inside the house worked well, she was essentially stuck indoors.

Until Clair arrived one bright summer morning.

Exhausted from caring for Bethany all night, I still wore my bathrobe. I cracked the door open and tightened my robe as I saw two men standing in the yard. Clair was at the door, grinning with that wide smile we'd come to appreciate in our church congregation. He and two other retired construction workers had taken on a much-needed volunteer ministry — building wheelchair ramps.

I stared at the stack of wood they'd already laid in the yard in disbelief.

ELAINE MARIE COOPER

"Didn't they tell you I was coming?" He smiled even bigger, if that were possible.

"No. But thank you!" I remembered my attire. "I'll be out in a minute — let me get dressed."

I closed the door, hurried upstairs to my bedroom, and threw on some clothes.

"Bethany!" I was so excited I yelled at her from the stairwell. "They're making you a wheelchair ramp! You'll get to go out!"

Bethany's grin almost matched Clair's.

The three workers constructed the ramp in record time. It extended more than twenty feet from our front steps down to our walkway and was constructed for us as a gift — completely free of charge.

As the smooth path to freedom for Bethany formed that day, we talked about where we might go. It had opened up all manner of possibilities. We could take her out to eat. Go to movies. Just go for a drive. The possibilities seemed limitless in that moment.

Who would have thought that wood, hammer, and nails would bring such a sense of hope and freedom? It was not the first time those same tools inspired liberty. The same items were essential to obtain freedom from our sins on the cross.

Perhaps it was no coincidence that Jesus was the son of a carpenter.

Note to self: No matter how tired you are, always get dressed first thing in the morning.

Note to others: In God's eyes, there is no such thing as retirement from ministry. Clair worked for Jesus until the day he died. What a precious servant.

25

"He got saved! Ben got saved! I am so privileged to serve a living God who has heard my prayers and reached down to pull the blindfold off of my brother. I am SO glad!! I will never have to worry about his wellbeing again because he will know the Father!! He can live a life of hope and die a death of triumph. If I died right now I would die completely fulfilled and satisfied that I could serve my God!!!! This is what makes life worth living."

— Bethany's Diary, July 28, 1996

While Bethany's brother Nate had been home frequently, her older brother, Ben, had been in navy flight school in Florida. As her condition was declining, I knew Ben needed to come home for a visit.

The day came when I called him and laid out the picture. "If you don't come now, I don't know how much longer she'll be able to interact with you." Ben was taken by surprise, but took my words to heart. He arranged for a flight home within the month.

Bethany could not wait to see him. Both her brothers converged at the house on the same weekend, bringing lots of noise and joy. That Sunday, the boys prepared to go to church.

My daughter hated missing service, but she was too weak to go. She loved singing "Here I am to Worship" by Tim Hughes, and would bemoan the fact that the praise and worship team might sing it, and she would miss that song. So Bethany and I would sing the words together at home. They were words of worship that declared the awesomeness of a God worthy of praise and honor. The lines about the beauty of the Lord and His devotion to us in this life always leave me in reverential wonder.

I am still amazed that in her frail physical state her spirit could rise above the circumstances to sing these words from her heart.

Every time I hear this song, I think of it as "Bethany's Song."

So as the boys prepared to attend church with Steve, I requested they pick up donuts afterwards as a treat. I neglected to include one detail — only buy one donut per person.

It sounds like a minor detail — except they brought home a dozen donuts! My eyes widened at the display, anticipating trouble ahead with Bethany's now-voracious appetite. Between the brain tumor and her medications, she craved food all the time. She had gained a lot of weight. This would not have been as much of a problem except that with my bad back, physically helping her was becoming more difficult. And she needed more help all the time.

Trying not to make a big deal out of the dozen donuts, I cautioned Ben to put the box in the kitchen, out of Bethany's sight.

We thought all was well — until a few minutes later I saw her walking out of that room with another donut in hand, ready to devour it. Apparently the knowledge that donuts were in the house had rallied her energy enough to walk all the way into the kitchen.

"Bethany, can we put that away till later?"

"But I want it now." She could be childlike in her illness.

"Well, really, we need to not eat more than one donut at a time. Maybe later, as a treat." I gently took the donut from her and wrapped it up until later in the day. I put all the donuts up high in the cupboard. I hoped she wouldn't try to climb up on the counter. A few minutes later, Ben joined me in the kitchen, smothering a laugh.

"What?" I grinned at his expression.

He kept his voice low. "When she came into the living room, she pouted and said, 'I could've had another donut.'"

We both covered our mouths to keep from laughing.

Nate and I visited together in the family room while Ben sat next to his sister in the living room. Our house is wide open, which is nice for having guests over, but not so nice if you want a private conversation. This time, I was glad I was able to listen in on Ben and Bethany's chat.

He was telling her about learning to fly aircraft and what the experience was like. She sat in a comfortable recliner and listened with rapt attention, occasionally asking questions. It was obvious she delighted in his company as well as his stories about the navy life.

Then she spoke words to her older brother that I will never forget. Words that still bring tears to my eyes.

"Someday," she said, "when I'm up in heaven, I'm going to look down at you flying an airplane and tell everyone, 'Look. There's my brother.'"

It is a memory I will always treasure.

Note to self: "Youths may faint and grow weary, and young men stumble and fall, but those who trust in the LORD will renew their strength; they will soar on wings like eagles; they will run and not grow weary; they will walk and not faint." — Isaiah 40:30-31

Note to others: Don't delay visiting those who the Lord draws you to see. You never know if it might be your last opportunity to be with them this side of eternity.

26

"Life really is good. I love it when I have time to stop and smell the roses....The Father has given me more time to spend with Him, making the rest of the day that much sweeter. He is so good to give me this time on the mountain so that I will be able to get through the valleys that lie ahead."

— *Bethany's Diary, June 6, 1995*

My perennial garden was my therapy. When Bethany slept, I would throw on my gloves and dig in the dirt out front, stabbing at weed roots and tossing the offending interlopers into a bin.

If only I could have gotten rid of the roots of cancer in my daughter's head so easily. But at least by attacking the ground outside, I could take out my frustration where it would actually be beneficial — in my weed-filled yard. Surgery had been ineffective for my daughter's tumor. But surgically extracting weeds out of my garden served to help me physically and emotionally.

I had other outlets as well. For me, crocheting and cross-stitching were helpful projects on which to focus my attention.

Even today, whenever I look at the frayed strands of thread on the back of aida cloth used for cross-stitch, I think of the comparison of a beautiful needlework project with God's view of our lives. He can see the gorgeous finished piece from heaven while our perspective here on earth is the unkempt mass of shredded embroidery floss on the back. The back is never the preferred side. But from the heavenly perspective, I believe that Bethany's life during her illness had taken on the image of a glorious piece of art. Even on the underside of a life filled with cancer, I can still see her beauty.

Everyone needs an outlet for their pain when taking care of a loved one who is seriously ill or dying. Some might choose working out, running, or dancing. Others might toss pots on a potter's wheel. But whatever the interest, it is the combination of physical and mental concentration on another activity that can help release the stress of the situation.

And then there is the need to cry. It's pretty tough to let down your guard in front of your patient.

I personally became adept at crying while driving alone. My tears would be further fueled when tuning in to the Christian radio station. Inevitably, the then-current hit "God is God" by Steven Curtis Chapman would come on, reminding me that I can't see God's bigger picture. And He is God, after all. Not me.

With the number of car trips I made, wearing sunglasses and tears streaming down my face, it's a wonder I never got pulled over for a DWW — Driving While Wailing.

There are times when a parent in such a situation needs counseling. Don't ever be afraid to access a counselor who can minister to your emotional and spiritual needs.

I sought grief counseling through hospice after Bethany passed away. But there is no one size fits all for emotional needs during a family crisis. Try not to be so overwhelmed with your tasks that you ignore your heart. A soul weighted down by grief lacks energy to do the most basic caregiving. Feed your soul as well as your body. You need all the strength you can muster.

Note to self: "My flesh and my heart may fail, but God is the strength of my heart, my portion forever." — Psalm 73:26

Note to others: While friends can be wonderful as listening ears, sometimes an impartial counselor can be a better source for helping you through the rough spots. Friends and family members may not be emotionally equipped to offer sound counseling. And sometimes there are things you might find too difficult to share with someone close. Seek a professional counselor. Never hesitate to get help wherever you need it. Just because you have faith doesn't eliminate the need for help, and needing help doesn't make you a weak Christian.

27

"How good and precious is our Lord Who answers our cries; yet often they are answered in such unobvious, unexpected ways that we miss His answer."

— Bethany's Diary, August 25, 1996

I had never picked out a casket before. I certainly never thought that when I did, it would be for my child.

It was a surreal visit, Steve and I sitting with the funeral director. He went through the list of items available for purchase, such as guest book, programs, and liners for caskets.

Then we toured the showroom of boxes meant to hold a person's remains. There were metal ones, colored ones, simple pine caskets.

Is this really happening?

I guessed it must be because I kept tearing up, and the funeral director kept wiping his moist eyes. The tissue box was passed around a few times.

As difficult as this was, the thought of waiting and going through this after Bethany passed away was inconceivable. It would be impossible to deal with emotionally. It was difficult enough doing it before the fact. Then the funeral director asked us the question that stumped both Steve and me.

"Where will she be buried?"

We sat there in silence.

Finally, someone spoke. Was it Steve or I? I do not recollect.

"We have no idea."

We had been in Iowa for fourteen years, but we didn't have a family plot. Where indeed? How do you decide that?

The funeral director suggested a few locations, even encouraging us to visit various cemeteries to get a feel for each possible resting place.

"Do you have a dog?"

What an odd question.

"Yes. But why?"

"Take the dog with you. If they're comfortable, then you'll be comfortable."

That was a new suggestion to me.

We shook hands and he squeezed ours. I was sure he'd done this many times before. But I'm sure it doesn't get any easier — especially when it's parents burying a child.

We walked outside stone-faced. Too bad we weren't really made out of granite. Then our hearts wouldn't be breaking.

Years before, I had read an article in the newspaper about a historic cemetery out in the countryside. I was attracted to it, not just because I love history but because it was started by the Irish, which is part of my lineage.

I hadn't thought about this place in a long time, but it beckoned me now to check it out. Calling the cemetery caretaker, I arranged to meet him there.

Steve had to work that day, but my dear friends, Laura and Peggy, were available to stay with Bethany. I didn't tell Bethany where I was going so I left the dogs at home, lest she wonder why I was taking them. With weighted heart, I drove south to the countryside.

Travelling over a dusty gravel road, past pastures filled with cows and an occasional house, my eyes were drawn to the site sitting high on a hill. The cemetery was beautiful, considering it was a place where the dead reside.

I parked the car and strolled over the dry grass in between the grave markers. Ancient tombstones stood side-by-side with newer slabs of granite. Old gravestone etchings shared stories of tragedies that had happened to the very young as well as the old.

I'm not the only parent to have lost a child.

The rugged caretaker, who was also a fulltime farmer, arrived and shook my hand with a firm grip. He explained where there were available plots. I thanked him and told him I'd look around.

Needing to be alone, I wandered off by myself to pray. I was far away from the man when I silently spoke to my Creator.

Lord, how am I supposed to know where to place my daughter? How do you decide where your child should be buried? Help me, Lord.

What happened next is still vivid in my mind.

A butterfly floated down in front of me, fluttering wispy strokes as it slowly landed on the ground not far away. I walked with measured steps toward the delicate creature, not wanting to disturb it. I gazed at the wings that moved several times in slow symmetry. After a long moment, during which I stared in rapt amazement, the creature flew away. I never saw it again.

I looked at the spot upon which it had landed and memorized its location. I looked up where the caretaker was and yelled, "Over here."

He strode toward the incline facing east.

"Here. This is where I want my daughter buried."

"Right here?"

"Yes." I told him the story about the butterfly. He eyed me with the quiet courtesy of an Iowa farmer. I'm not certain the man believed me.

But I knew what I had seen.

The caretaker made notes as I silently thanked God for showing me the way — and the place.

As I finished the business I had come to do, I turned to walk back to the car.

I looked around for the butterfly — any butterfly — but it was nowhere to be seen. And then I realized something.

I had not seen any butterflies on that country hillside before or after — the entire day.

After Bethany died and I ordered her tombstone, I made sure they put an etching on the granite of a daisy, her favorite flower. Right next to the daisy I had them carve a butterfly in memory of my winged visitor that day.

Note to self: Even walking an unfamiliar, lonely path is made more bearable by the presence of your always familiar Friend.

Note to others: Sometimes working in tandem to help a caregiver makes the burden easier for friends. By coming together to help Bethany, my friends Laura and Peggy could bolster each other in the difficult task while bolstering my spirits by being dependable caregivers. I am so grateful to all my friends who were such a blessing during this time.

28

"What's going to happen to me? Nobody knows except God. And really, the One Who brought me here will bring me through. I cannot hang onto my ideas of what my body should be, what my mind should hold, or what my being should accomplish. The longer I hold to these past images, the harder this new life is going to be. It will be the life of God's choosing."

— *Bethany's Diary, February 2, 2002*

*S*ummer had ended and school started up once again. This year, my job had switched from substitute school nurse to fulltime nurse at an elementary school.

It was a strange time to be starting a new job, but it was much-needed provision for our family. Bethany's two insurances covered the cost of fulltime caregivers to stay with her during the day. My workday ended by three o'clock so I could get home early to be with her.

By now she was bed-bound, unable to manage even basic moving around on her own. Her weak muscles and lack of coordination put her at risk for falling, so her hospital bed provided a safe place.

We set up a TV in her room and tried to make it as cheerful as possible. Friends and family called or visited, but speaking became more and more difficult and talking on the phone was taxing for her.

Mom came over and would spend time visiting with her. Two of her cousins from California, James and Joanne, came for a visit.

The morning they were going to see her, Bethany had a terrible headache, so I begged the cousins to be patient until we could get the pain under control. They understood completely and waited for me to call them. Finally in the afternoon, the intensity of Bethany's pain subsided, and I was able to invite them over. The cousins had a great visit together. Bethany rose to the occasion, laughing and interacting with them for an hour or more.

After they left, her efforts at socializing had obviously exhausted her. Bethany always tried to be at her best when others were there, despite the fact that she tired easily. We were so grateful that her cousins took the time to visit.

In the midst of this downward slope, I worked every day at the school. Another school nurse asked me if I wished that everyone knew what was happening in my family so that others could sympathize with me.

I said "No." She seemed surprised but I explained. "When I'm here at school, I can pretend my life is completely normal, even though I know it's completely not normal. For a few hours I can just be a regular school nurse. When I go home, I have to face the difficulty. But school is my respite."

She understood. And while others in my situation might react differently, that was my way of surviving.

A teacher at my school who knew about Bethany was very kind. "I bet you wish you could be with your daughter all the time."

I looked at her and replied in all honesty. "No. It's too hard. It was one thing to be with her all the time when she was young and growing stronger. But now she's growing weaker and it's so difficult to watch." She understood as well.

If I never got a break from the pain, I would not have the stamina to ever smile or be the loving mom I needed to be. And if I was with her all the time, and then one day she was gone, how would I survive with the emptiness?

Yet I knew the emptiness was coming.

How will I survive when she is gone?

Note to self: "I called on Your name, Yahweh, from the depths of the Pit. You hear my plea: Do not ignore my cry for relief. You come near when I call You; You say: 'Do not be afraid.'" — Lamentations 3:55-57

Note to others: Were you ever surprised by the reaction of someone in a difficult emotional or physical storm? Be open to their voice with ears that truly hear. Be slow to judge and quick to understand.

"This is what the Lord has been pressing on my heart: That I would love Him fully, completely, and consistently. See, I know I believe in His Word and am in love with Him now, but with the vast, uncertain future looming ahead I cannot help but cry to my Father that my love for Him might never waver...With His help I can stay not only a servant all my days, but a slave who is not capable of deserting her worthy Master. Please, my Lord, don't let me leave!"

— *Bethany's Diary, August 4, 1996*

Can one die from exhaustion?

I feared it could happen. I feared it would happen to me. *Lord, please keep me alive at least long enough to be here for Bethany. Give me the strength that seems to elude me.*

Every morning I dragged myself from my bed at four o'clock. Besides getting myself ready for work, Steve and I had to change Bethany. It took two of us, as her weak muscles rendered her unable to help.

I remember one morning when my nerves were raw, and Steve was complaining about how tired he was. I snapped.

"Get out!" Flames of anger and fatigue heated my words. "We don't need you. I'll take care of her myself. Get out!"

He quickly changed his tone. "You can't do this alone."

"Yes, I can." My determination was stronger than the reality of the situation. I wasn't strong enough to do this alone, but in that moment, I didn't care. I was so upset and spent. We finished caring for her and I picked up dirty linens and left.

It was not a great start to the day.

But God was gracious and we survived that temporary crisis. Asking forgiveness of each other, we understood the terrible stress we were both under. We were both exhausted and, despite my explosive words, we recovered from our argument.

We were in this together and God was our strength. It was obvious that Bethany's health was declining, and the stress was enormous.

But venting in front of our daughter was not helpful for her, nor a godly solution to our situation. We needed to make things right with her as well.

Bethany wasn't used to hearing us argue like that, so we had to apologize and reassure her that all would be fine and we were there for her. Together.

I found a piece of paper she had written on a few weeks prior, when she could still write. She was declining and she obviously knew it. The paper said something like this… "I hope they will take care of me."

If words ever tore at a parent's heart, those words shredded mine.

After I saw that note, I reassured her. "Of course we'll take care of you. As long as you need us, you will be here in our home with us and you will be cared for."

I'm sure she wondered if we could manage, and I'm certain she knew there was a residential facility nearby. While that is the only option for some families with a dying loved one, it was not an option for Steve or me. Bethany was always so confused about things as it was. Imagine her confusion if we sent her away.

The thought left me cold. As her parents, the thought was unacceptable. If she was going to die, the only destination we wanted for her after living in our home was living in heaven.

Note to self: "The fruit of the Spirit is love, joy, peace, patience, kindness, goodness, faith, gentleness, self-control. Against such things there is no law. Now those who belong to Christ Jesus have crucified the flesh with its passions and desires. If we live by the Spirit, we must also follow the Spirit. We must not become conceited, provoking one another, envying one another." — Galatians 5:22-26

Note to others: Sometimes caregivers need one-on-one time with a friend to talk about their frustrations. Taking a caregiver out for coffee and allowing them to express their frustrations and fears is a way to help them express those thoughts out of earshot of a patient. A venting with a *vente.*

30

"There is beauty in each moment. There is the hand of God in each one. It may not always be obvious, but to a trained eye, it is visible. Look to the One Who gave me my moments and you, your moments, and everyone one of them will become as valuable as pure gold. After all, it will only be a matter of moments before this life is through and others are experiencing their moments. Then, I won't have to worry about moments. It will be one long, glorious, eternal moment spent in the love of God."

— Bethany's Diary, August 26, 1995

Bethany's favorite dessert was colorful dots of flash frozen ice cream, eaten with a spoon. The trouble was, they were only available at one location — a local theme park. Much to our daughter's delight, her hospice worker Dorothy managed to secure several servings for Bethany. Dorothy had them delivered to our home. The treats came preserved in dry ice, and so we had a party in a hospital bed. Dorothy's kindness and care is forever imbedded in our hearts and memories.

Sandy, Bethany's nurse, was coming over more frequently that early October. She continued to engage us with her bubbly personality, but it was obvious that Bethany was weakening.

In private, Sandy explained to me the tumor would continue to grow, eventually reaching her brain stem. Then it would only be a matter of time.

Sandy gave me a book that described firsthand experiences of caregivers with their dying loved ones. She didn't have to explain why she had given it to me.

Reading it from cover to cover, I learned about the variety of near-death and dying chronicles of many others who had walked in the shoes I now wore. It was new territory for me in my limited experience with death. Even though I am a nurse, my patients were usually well or recovering. The closest I had come to being with a dying person was taking a young mom who had just delivered a premature baby to the neonatal intensive care unit (NICU) where her infant daughter died in her arms. That was an unforgettable experience.

How would I cope with my own daughter's death? I had no answers. All I could do was trust the Lord would see me through this.

In reading the book Sandy provided, it described how sometimes dying patients see other people most of us cannot see. Sometimes patients would talk about seeing others who had died long ago.

Then I recalled a story I'd heard years before. In George Gallup's *Adventures in Immortality*, (1983) the author relates a story told by Billy Graham when he was at the deathbed of his grandmother. Suddenly sitting up in bed, his grandmother described seeing her husband who had died years before. Her spouse had been a veteran of the Civil War and had lost a leg and an eye in that conflict. According to Billy Graham, his grandmother claimed to be seeing her husband, his body restored with both legs and eyes, just before she entered eternity. These stories amazed me. They also helped prepare me for things Bethany began to say.

One day when Sandy and I walked into her room, Bethany started talking about someone.

"There's a man sitting up there on the…" She began to wave her hands as if to point. She couldn't describe what he was on. "He's a blond man. He's watching me and smiling."

Sandy and I stared where Bethany was pointing. We saw no one. Bethany continued. "He seems to know things."

We tried not to be surprised and accepted Bethany's words without denying her reality. When Bethany described the man as having blond hair, Sandy blurted out, "Oooo, kind of like that angel on *Touched By an Angel!*"

Bethany narrowed her eyes. "Sandy, you've been watching way too much TV."

We burst out laughing at her comment. Bethany's humor seemed to always survive when much else did not.

Then Bethany said something else surprising. "There are people with you."

"With me?" Confusion fluttered through my thoughts.

"Yes. There's a young Hispanic woman with you, Mom."

"Really?"

What is still amazing to me is that I was not made uncomfortable or fearful by her words. Perhaps she was seeing others we could not see. And if she was, I would not dismiss her observations as drug-induced hallucinations.

I had too much respect for Bethany. And for God.

Note to self: "Now to which of the angels has He ever said: Sit at My right hand until I make Your enemies Your footstool? Are they not all ministering spirits sent out to serve those who are going to inherit salvation?" — Hebrews 1:13-14

Note to others: "...by Him everything was created, in heaven and on earth, the visible and the invisible, whether thrones or dominions or rulers or authorities — all things have been created through Him and for Him." — Colossians 1:16

31

"Lord, please help me to love them as you do."

— *Bethany's Diary, July 19, 1996*

"Mom, I'm worried about Steven."

My thoughts jerked away from the ever-present concern for my daughter's well being.

"You're worried about Steven?"

Who could think about anyone else at the moment? All I could ponder was my daughter's needs.

She looked at me from her hospital bed in her bedroom, her gaze earnest and her voice concerned. "Mom, Steven doesn't believe in God. He doesn't think there is a God. I'm worried I won't see him in heaven."

I was speechless. I hadn't thought about Steven in weeks. "Well, I guess we need to pray for him."

Sure. Later. Right now I'm worried about you. Steven is about the last person on my mind.

"Yeah." Bethany closed her eyes, her energy sapped.

Later, I sat by her bedside. It was after work and dinner was over. Bethany appeared to be resting, but I just wanted to be near her — while I still could. I sat there without speaking, wishing I could hold her hand or stroke her arm. But lately, even touching her seemed to cause discomfort. So I held my own hands together, pondering what the future held. Dreading what the future held.

I thought she was asleep when she suddenly opened her eyes wide. "My body is going to stop functioning."

Lifting my head up, my eyes narrowed as I stared at her without knowing what to say. How do you reply to such a statement from your child, even if you know it's true?

"I'm going to die." She began to cry softly.

Tears poured from my eyes as I tenderly touched her hand. "Bethany." It was the only thing I could think to say. We wept together as I told her how much I would miss her. How much I loved her.

I do not recall much after that. Some things are just too painful to remember.

Later, I told Sandy what Bethany had said to me.

"She's giving you a gift. She's preparing you."

Leave it to Bethany to think of others at such a time.

The constant whirr of the oxygen condenser became the background music for our home. A long tube stretched from the front room to the back bedroom, where the comforting air flowed to Bethany's nose through thin, soft plastic tubing.

Occasional visits by caregivers and nurses only slightly interrupted Bethany's otherwise quiet moments. Her voice became weaker and weaker, making it difficult to understand her words. One afternoon, I could hear her murmuring. I leaned my ear closer to her and said, "What, Bethany?"

I heard her whisper, "I'm not finished flying south yet."

Confused, I gently squeezed her arm and kissed her cheek. "Okay."

Nate came home from St. Louis. He knew his sister was not long for this world. My heart broke even further knowing he would be saying goodbye to his forever friend.

The hospice volunteer, Roberta, hurried to see Bethany when she returned from vacation. After visiting in the bedroom, Roberta came out to see me in the dining room. Her face was drawn and her voice strained. "You know she doesn't have long."

Swallowing my heart in my throat, I answered, "I know."

Bethany became unresponsive to our voices. Then the rattling in her lungs started. It was loud and beyond unnerving.

I rarely phoned the on-call hospice nurse during the evening but I knew this was the beginning of the end.

The nurse asked me a few clinical questions, but she did not seem to think anything was imminent.

"Listen to her!" I walked into the bedroom and held the phone where the on-call nurse could hear what I was hearing.

The nurse was adamant. "It just sounds like she's snoring."

I walked out of Bethany's room, barely able to keep my irritation to myself. "She's not snoring." I wanted to throw something — preferably at the sleepy-sounding nurse.

"Well, call me if anything changes."

Right. You mean like, if she dies.

I raged silently but hung up the phone without resorting to the curses I felt welling in my thoughts.

Okay. I guess we are in this alone, Steve and Nate and I.

I will never leave you or forsake you.

Still small voices seemed unable to crack their way into my grieving heart. I told Steve the nurse wasn't coming and wished that Sandy had been on call that night. She would have come.

We kept our vigil by Bethany's side. I desperately fought the urge to stroke her arm, knowing it seemed to be an irritant. I could only imagine the chaos occurring in her nervous system, making any stimulation painful.

Checking her temperature under her arm, I nearly dropped the thermometer. 106.6. I had never seen such a fever before. Sandy had told us that Bethany's temperature would become out of control once the tumor had made it's ugly advance.

So we waited. Looking at Nate's face, my maternal pain leaped to immeasurable proportions.

"Nate, why don't you go rest? We'll stay here and call if we need you."

He reluctantly stood up, kissed his sister, and went into his old bedroom to get much-needed sleep.

Steve and I sat by her bedside. The rattling sound was so persistent, but she still hung on. Who knew for how long? We vacillated between wanting it to stop and hoping she would stay.

My eyelids drooped. "Hon, I need to go lay down on the sofa. I'll set the alarm for two hours, then you can go sleep. Call me if you need me."

"Okay."

Dragging myself away from Bethany's bedside, I found the alarm clock and set it for five o'clock. I collapsed on the sofa and was asleep when I hit the pillow.

The alarm went off in the early morning darkness. I slammed it off and sat up. I could still hear the rattling in the other room and went in to relieve Steve.

While he went to bed, I sat by my dying daughter. The rattling had increased, and I knew her lungs were filling up with fluid.

Lord, help her not be in pain!

She did not seem to be in need of morphine. We gave it to her in small drops under her tongue when she appeared agitated. But now she was still. Even so, I wished there was something I could do.

I went in the other room and called Sandy. When I told her what was going on, she never hesitated. "I'll be right there."

Returning to the bedside vigil, the death rattle seemed to increase in volume. It was horrible, loud, and so persistent I finally burst into tears. Great sobs waved through me as I felt I could not stand anymore.

God help me. God help her.

Just then, Bethany's breathing slowed down. Then it stopped. I looked at the clock. 6:07 a.m. Then one more breath. 6:08 a.m., October 20, 2003. My daughter was in the hands of Jesus.

Her glassy eyes remained open. I gently swept her lids downward, closing her view of this world forever.

Bethany's calendar here on earth was now complete.

Note to self: "Be strong and courageous; don't be terrified or afraid of them. For it is the Lord your God who goes with you; He will not leave you or forsake you." — Deuteronomy 31:6

Note to others: The memory of being alone with my daughter when she died still pains me. I suppose I could have called the nurse back, but her lack of response with my first call left me distrustful. I wasn't going to beg. In my heart I truly forgive her, but my memory of being alone with Bethany as she took her last breath is a deeply painful one that still hurts. One can forgive, even when the mind cannot forget.

Although the nurse let me down that dark night, I know God was with me all along, holding me close and ministering to me. People may fail us, but God never does. "He heals the brokenhearted and binds up their wounds." — Psalm 147:3

32

"One day the Master came and beckoned me aside. 'It's time for you to leave,' He told me. 'Your work here is finished, and now it's time for you to go to another field.'

'No, my Lord!' I cried as I sunk to my knees. 'I know this field and all its idiosyncrasies. I love this field and my fellow workers. Please don't send me to a cold, foreign place where I am all alone.'

'You don't understand.' He refuted. 'You are never going to be alone, for I will be with you always. You no longer serve Me best here. Your work in the next field will bring Me an even greater harvest, and you will please Me by working where I choose you to work. It will be even better there.'

I nodded in agreement as He took my hand gently in His and we began walking the trail to the next field. My eyes welled with tears as I felt all that was familiar slip behind me with each step toward my new field. All the while, however, I kept my gaze steadily on my Master's glorious face. I never looked back because I knew that to do so would be failing to trust Him and His assurance that He would be with me.

The longer we walked, the more absorbing His beauty became and, after awhile, I ceased recognition of anything but His Glory. I forgot the other field and all of its beloved inhabitants. I simply gazed into His face. As if we had never even left our previous dwelling, I realized that we had arrived. And just as my Master had promised, it was even more amazing than I imagined it could be."

— From Bethany's Diary when she left home for college, August 28, 1996

I had never before had to choose an outfit for a person who was going to be buried. I was grateful Nate was there to help me.

Choosing a lovely lavender blouse and a skirt, I walked around the department store with Nate, wondering what to put on her feet. It didn't really matter. It just didn't feel right to leave her feet bare.

Much to my surprise Nate came over to me holding a pair of socks and grinning.

"Bethany would love these."

I was a bit bewildered by his choice — long, fuzzy, purple monkey socks.

"Monkey socks?" I didn't know whether to laugh or cry.

He reiterated, "She would love these."

I put aside my notions of formal dress and had to agree. "You're right — she would love these." No one knew Bethany like her little brother.

We delivered the attire to the funeral home — formal blouse, ankle length skirt, and monkey socks. No one would see them. But it put a smile on our face to know they were there.

Ben arrived home from flight school within a day. The following day, his girlfriend, Kristen, also arrived from Georgia to bid Bethany goodbye. She and Bethany had never met, but they knew about each other. What Bethany did not know was that Kristen would be her future sister-in-law.

We scheduled three events to honor Bethany's memory — a visitation at the funeral home, a graveside service the following day, and a memorial service the next day. Looking back, I would have arranged the sequence on two days. By the third day, while awaiting the start of the service to celebrate Bethany's life, I confided to my future daughter-in-law, "I wish this was over."

Hundreds of friends and family showed up to the visitation service to pay their respects. A long line of church friends, relatives, and co-workers wove through the room. The smile plastered on my face belied the pain coursing through my heart. I think I said all the right things a grieving mother is supposed to say. But no one says the honest words really dwelling in their mind: How will I survive this?

The next day was a clear, but cool October morning. A small group of close family and friends gathered at the graveside out in the Iowa countryside. I pulled my black crocheted shawl closer around my shoulders as I shivered from a cool breeze. Pastor Todd asked if I was alright.

"Sure, I'm fine."

We dutifully sat on the fold up chairs lined along the length of the pine casket. Todd opened his Bible and began to speak briefly about Bethany and her soul now in heaven. While currently one of our church pastors, Todd had known Bethany since she was in high school, and he was her youth pastor. He had been a witness to her faith since before her illness.

The beautiful service on this bright, crisp morning was serene and sad. After the brief eulogy, we all stood up together and spoke little. The quietness enveloped us all as we pondered the life of Bethany, now alive in heaven.

Suddenly, the stillness was interrupted with an unexpected sight. Three Canada geese, flying in V-formation, flew directly over our grieving group. It was startling, not just due to their loud honking, but because they were flying so low and right over our heads.

We stared in wonder and awe, and felt the closeness of both Bethany as well as her Creator. It was a magical and comforting moment.

Returning to our home, we fed the group of visitors — mostly family — with the abundance of fare provided by neighbors and church friends. We sat around reminiscing about good times and reading enjoyable excerpts from one of her childhood diaries. I distributed several CD's to her friends — music Bethany had listened to during her illness. Even today, I cannot listen to Caedmon's Call or Michael W. Smith's worship CD without thinking of Bethany. It is still a painful memory, even after so many years.

The weather the next morning was cold and rainy. I praised God the graveside service the previous day had been sunny. Now, on this last day of remembering Bethany in a formal service, the skies wept with us.

Bethany had chosen the songs she wanted played at her funeral. Even now, I still am in awe that God gave her and I the strength to have that discussion when she was still able to make those decisions. She picked out three songs — "I Can Only Imagine" by Mercy Me, "North of the Sky" by East to West, and "How Beautiful" to be sung by one of her favorite church vocalists, Laura Deever.

Friends and family from far and wide came to Des Moines. Steve collected written memories from several of them and shared their thoughts at the celebration of life service.

Here are a few of the memories that were shared…

College friend Lisa Baughman — "This is my favorite memory of Bethany: Our jokes that no one seemed to think were funny except us. Bethany's sense of endless humor is what I will miss the most. Even while in the hospital waiting to get her blood drawn a few months ago, when Elaine went to see what the holdup was, Bethany whispered to me, 'Mom's gonna go put the smack down on 'em.' I will forever love my dear friend Bethany. Her smile and laugh, quick wit, intelligence, drive, wisdom, incredible faith, sense of adventure and fun, and her deep love for people will continue to teach and inspire me for the rest of my life. She was, and will continue to be, a rare treasure to those who had the privilege to know her."

College friend, Julie Merritt, remembered their dorm room "Broadway" performances with post-show "interviews." "Bethany was the field correspondent conducting the interview. Some of her most memorable questions (always using a hairbrush microphone) were, 'So, Lisa, this performance seems to deviate from your usual repertoire. Can you speak to this?' or 'I noticed that one of your pieces was a little darker than most of your other choices. Why is that, Julie?' Bethany would conduct the interview with a professionalism that was second-to-none and her deadpan humor had us rolling!"

College friend, Kristen Vibbert, remembered Bethany's fake reading glasses to help her study. She also treasured the trip that Kathryn, Bethany, and she took to Edinburgh, Scotland, "when Kathryn and Nard (Bethany's nickname) told BAD jokes the whole time." Kristen's list of favorites included: "Nard's total calm for four years whenever I was stressing about papers, tutorials, or comps; Bethany dancing Topol's part from *Fiddler on the Roof.*" And number one on Kristen's list of favorite memories? "Bethany's laugh."

College friend, Ann Pittman — "What I remember most about Bethany is her encouraging attitude. She always seemed genuinely concerned about how others and I were doing. She loved her friends, and that was always evident by the encouragement she gave us. I will remember her smiles that sometimes seemed to originate from some faraway place, and I will remember her laugh."

Dr. Ken Chatlos, professor at William Jewel College — "I taught Bethany in the introductory Oxbridge tutorial. From that time on, she and I visited periodically about common interests. One of those interests concerned care for the elderly in nursing homes…One day Bethany and I were chatting about these matters, and I suggested that she join us (my wife and I) for a trip up to Chillicothe to the Baptist Home for the Aged. There, I told her, she would see a first rate nursing home, which tended to the physical and spiritual lives of its residents. Bethany's reply: 'When?' …I thought often of this trip, particularly during my regular prayers for Bethany. I have invited other students to join me for the trip, but your daughter is the only one so far to take me up on this offer."

Faithful friend Sarah Johnson, who accompanied Bethany on an outing near the late stages of her illness – "The day I will remember most with Bethany is the day we went to Adventureland. Bethany was so happy to be there. I had a wonderful time, and it was so good to share the day with Bethany and Steve. I remember how excited she was about her brand new tennis shoes. I will never forget riding the Space Shot. She seemed a little hesitant at first, but she rode it anyway. After the ride was over, she said she liked it a lot. The best part of the day was just getting to spend it with her. It was such a blessing to me, and I will never forget it.

One of the best memories I will always carry with me is how she made me feel whenever I'd come to visit her. She always seemed so happy to see me, and I always felt incredibly loved when I saw her. No matter how she was feeling, she had a big smile and a hug to greet me."

From Bethany's Dad, Steve — "The other day, I was flipping through a scrapbook that Bethany put together at the end of her senior year in high school, and I came across an interesting list that Bethany made of words that she felt described her. Bethany said that she was… Confident, motivated, sincere, analytical, serious, different, and busy.

"I'd completely agree with her list and perhaps add a few traits. She was also, as we've heard, very funny and fun loving. She was graceful and faithful — that is, full of grace and faith. She was inquisitive, compassionate, determined, wise, witty, and possessed a keen intellect. She was an enormous person in a small package.

She was something. Really something. She was a wonderful daughter. Beyond wonderful, really, somewhere that language cannot reach. I admit I am highly prejudiced about all this, of course. Because as her father, I loved her dearly and I will always love her dearly. I am tempted to tears and Elaine and I are in a time clouded with sadness. But the truth is: We are fortunate, very fortunate. Can you imagine the honor it was that God entrusted this precious life to us? She was amazing."

Note to self: "How beautiful on the mountains are the feet of the herald, who proclaims peace, who brings news of good things, who proclaims salvation, who says to Zion, 'Your God reigns!'" — Isaiah 52:7

Note to others: How beautiful in all the earth are the hands that bring good food, who proclaim words of comfort, who share words of hope in salvation through Jesus Christ; who say to the grieving, "Our God reigns!"

33

"Please hear what I am not saying. Why must I voice emotions buried so deeply that their excavations hurt more than they do?"

— *Bethany's Diary, August 24, 1996*

The grief counselor from hospice shared a story that helped her cope with the loss of her husband years before. In order to get through her day-to-day activities, she put her feelings of grief inside an imaginary fenced-in yard. After shutting and locking the gate, she would only visit "grief" at certain times, allowing her to function somewhat capably during the day when she was away from the fenced-in area.

This was a good illustration, one that helped me most of the time. But, of course, all the techniques in the world are not without their vulnerability. Broken pickets in the fence often allowed my unwanted grief to escape its supposed secure existence behind virtual bars of imprisonment. Sorrow seeped out frequently, often at unexpected times: Watching a mother laughing with her adult daughter while leaving a craft store; announcements of Mother-Daughter banquets at church; watching movies that I knew Bethany would have loved.

Grief always hovered just below the surface — an unwelcome visitor who knocked incessantly at my door.

Working all day as a school nurse gave meaning and purpose

to my life, and I was grateful for the children I could shower with my attention. They were mostly healthy with occasional broken bones or illnesses to tend. One day, a student's mother informed me that her son had been diagnosed with a brain tumor. This was not a scenario I had anticipated but, of course, was always a possibility with hundreds of students in my school. I hugged this young mother and told her I'd be praying for her and her family.

One more victim of this horrible disease.

After lunch one day, a teacher came to my office door. Speechless, she kept making hand motions and had a look of panic on her face. I quickly realized she was choking.

I got behind her and did the often practiced Heimlich maneuver. After several thrusts into her abdomen, the offending article dislodged, although I could not see anything. Her voice raspy, she informed the staff — who were standing there in terror — that she had been eating a french fry. It went down the wrong way, and she had run to my office for help.

I arranged for this teacher to be transported to the hospital to be further examined. Choking victims, even those who seem to recover, still need to see a doctor because of potential throat swelling.

After the teacher left for medical help, I breathed a huge sigh of relief.

Thank you, Jesus.

Later on, driving home, grief snuck out of the fenced in yard.

I could save a teacher, but I couldn't save my daughter.

Sobbing, I was grateful the teacher had survived, but felt like a failure that Bethany had not.

While the comparison between the two was obviously irrational, grief is not always reasonable.

My drive home from work often became my time to release the grief. I had held in my emotions all day. But when I put the key into the ignition and turned it on, the tears flowed along with the gasoline into the car engine.

There was one day I will never forget. Taking my usual route home from school, I drove by the apartment building where Bethany had lived prior to her diagnosis. While my crying was familiar, my audible complaint to God was not.

"Jesus, this is TOO HARD!" I yelled at him from my Subaru.

There was no audible reply. Just an inner voice I heard in my soul… *My grace is sufficient for you.*

The words startled me out of my sobs. I took a tissue and dried my eyes. It was a life-changing moment.

And while I continue to mourn over the loss of Bethany, I have never yelled at God since that day.

Note to self: "But He said to me, 'My grace is sufficient for you, for power is perfected in weakness.'" — 2 Corinthians 12:9

Note to others: Grief can last forever, this side of eternity. It can be worse at certain times like holidays and birthdays, but it is a constant, especially in the loss of a child. It can manifest itself in many ways, including depression and anger. If you know of someone who is grieving, try to be a listening ear without offering placating statements such as, "God never gives us more than we can handle." If a grieving friend seems to be overwhelmed, encourage them to seek professional counseling.

34

"*People are so lost! Without the grace of God they're just stumbling around in the world trying to make sense of it all. They're miserable because they're living half a life. They need heaven in their real world.*"

— *Bethany's Diary, September 1, 1995*

I t was now over a year since Bethany had died. That fact seemed surreal.

How could so many months have slipped away without my daughter? Didn't she just die yesterday?

Time takes on illogical dimensions after you lose a loved one.

In fact, it was a whole year plus several months after she had entered eternity that I felt prompted to paint her old bedroom upstairs.

Our family had carried on in as normal a manner as possible in the time since her death. Grief counselors refer to life after losing a loved one as the new normal. Nothing is quite ever the same — you adapt and adjust, but there is this vast hole in your family no one can fill.

We had a glimmer of joy the July after Bethany's death, when Ben and Kristen were married in a gorgeous Atlanta ceremony. Everyone was smiling. But, again, there was that void in our family pew on the groom's side. Perhaps Bethany watched from above. It was nice to think so.

My new daughter-in-law, Kristen, and her family had special

wreaths made from daisies, Bethany's favorite flower. They were placed on the church doors to commemorate her absence. It was a lovely and kind tribute we so appreciated.

Life would go on. And so would the ache in our hearts.

Since more than a year had now passed, I decided it was time to paint the bedroom that had once been Bethany's. I decided on a rich pink color that would reflect her personality — vibrant, romantic, sweet.

I prepared the room ahead of time, clearing off the papers from her desk and moving everything away from the walls.

Once the room was paint ready, I began to toss a plastic tarp over her desk. But a piece of paper caught my eye.

I put the plastic aside and picked up the small note. The handwriting was unfamiliar, but it had Steven's name and phone number on it.

Where did this come from?

I thought about a conversation months before with Jeanne, the coordinator of the care center where Bethany and Steven had met. Jeanne had taken Steven to Bethany's memorial service, but she told us later he was very angry about Bethany's death. How could God have taken her? Without faith, Steven's questions roiled in his spirit.

I remembered Bethany's concern about Steven. Would she see him in heaven?

Holding onto the small note, I took off my painting gloves and walked to the phone.

Lord, give me the words to say.

Steven answered after a few rings.

"Hey, Steven, this is Elaine Cooper, Bethany's Mom. How are you doing?"

"Hi."

I paused for a moment, looking for the right words. "I just

found your name and phone number on Bethany's desk. I don't even know who wrote it or how it got there, but I thought I'd call you. I hope you're doing all right."

"I'm doing OK."

"Well, hey, we're having a special service downtown this Sunday that our church is doing with a few other churches. If Steve and I picked you up, would you like to come with us?"

I waited for him to decline.

Instead, he said enthusiastically, "Yeah!"

I'm surprised I didn't drop the phone.

"Wonderful!" I gave him the time we'd pick him up. "See you Sunday!"

Hanging up the phone, I stood in disbelief for a moment. Then it hit me.

Steven's coming to church with us!

Practically doing the dance of joy, I phoned Steve at work to tell him the great news, then I picked up the paintbrush. It felt light as a feather as I stroked the walls with a fresh coat.

Lord, please do your work in Steven's heart.

But after hearing the young man's voice, I knew God's Spirit had already been hard at work.

We sat in the large auditorium designed to fit hundreds of people. We saw friends from other congregations whom we hadn't seen in months or years. It was like a great family reunion.

Introducing Steven to our friends, they all reached out their hands to him in welcome. Although he was among strangers, Steven's smile reflected the comfort that he was really among friends.

The music began and the singing was accompanied by clapping

to the beat. Steven enjoyed the upbeat music and participated with clapping, even if he didn't know the words to sing.

As the speaker began, Steven listened with rapt attention. Watching out of the corner of my eye, his posture expressed excitement. He seemed joyfully anxious as the minister neared the conclusion. When the opportunity was offered for anyone to come forward and pray, Steven seemed on the edge of his seat.

Leaning near him I said, "Do you want me to take you up to pray?"

"Yes!"

Standing up, I offered him my arm as he carried his white cane. We slowly went forward, and then behind a curtain. I approached one of the men whom I recognized.

"This is Steven and he'd like to pray."

My friend offered him a chair where they could talk. He spoke with Steven about faith in Jesus Christ and how He offers salvation to those who believe. Steven seemed more than ready to make a decision as he prayed to receive Christ.

Looking back on this moment, I can't help but believe that Bethany was singing and doing the Dance of Joy in heaven.

Or perhaps she was imitating Topol in *Fiddler on the Roof.*

That would be Bethany's style.

Note to all: "If you confess with your mouth, 'Jesus is Lord,' and believe in your heart that God raised Him from the dead, you will be saved. With the heart one believes, resulting in righteousness, and with the mouth one confesses, resulting in salvation." — Romans 10:9-10

35

Ten Years Later

Much has transpired in the ten years since Bethany went home to heaven.

Steven is doing well, still attends the care center, and still attends church with us on Sundays.

Ben and Kristen have blessed our families with three precious grandchildren. They faithfully serve the Lord in their local congregation.

Nate continues to be a joy in our lives. He currently lives in southern California and faithfully serves the Lord in a large area church.

Sarah met the love of her life — Chad — and they are now the blessed parents of three precious children. Sarah still works as a nurse, and we still go out for coffee together whenever we can.

My Mom died last August at the amazing age of ninety-nine. She is buried next to Bethany in the Irish Settlement Cemetery.

My husband, Steve, is still working as an editor, and our lives are busier than ever. While statistics say that the majority of marriages end after losing a child, I am so grateful we were in the minority. I credit Steve's patience, and the Lord's faithfulness.

On the fourth anniversary of Bethany's death, I lay in bed without any intentions of getting up. I wanted to cover my head and hide from the world. I hated these dates of remembrance.

But God had other plans for me that day. With an inaudible voice speaking to my heart, I "heard" a very strange assignment. I was to write a novel about my ancestors during the American Revolution. The message was so clear to me yet so strange that I was embarrassed to tell Steve.

After all, although I had previously been a freelance writer for newspapers and magazines, I was now a fulltime nurse. Besides, the only time I had tried to write after Bethany's death, I had melted into a pool of tears. I never wanted to write again.

And now I was being directed to write a historical novel. Okay, so I love history and family genealogy. But this made no sense.

Since our ways are not God's ways, I decided to go to the used bookstore and start looking for books about American history. And the rest became part of my history as one novel turned into two, then two turned into three.

I had already decided I would never write about Bethany.

Relive that pain? Never!

Again, God had other ideas.

It was at a Christian writers' conference in 2011 during praise and worship time when I felt the next heavenly nudge. I was to write Bethany's story and He would give me the strength to do it.

My tears strangled my singing as the reality of this new marching order sank into my spirit. Yet even as I wept, I knew it would be all right. Because He would be with me every step of the way as I recalled Bethany's story and wept once again for my loss.

And He has been faithful. He has been my rock.

Never fear the tears — only fear missing out on God's will for your life.

Things we learned...

For anyone who has a loved one with a serious illness, I pray the Lord uses our experiences to help you. My husband and I have compiled a list of suggestions we hope will help…

• Always carry a designated notebook and pen, or an electronic device, to take notes during all doctor and hospital visits. Write down the doctor's name and every piece of important information you might need. If you need a word clarified or spelled, stop the doctor and ask. If the doctor is rushed and leaves before all your questions are answered, ask his or her nurse.

• Keep an updated list of all the patient's medications, their dosage and frequency. Always carry a copy with you, in your purse or wallet, in case there is an emergency.

• Always update your patient's healthcare visits and pertinent information in one notebook or Word document on your computer. Note names of doctors, what they were seen for, and any new medications added at that visit.

• There are wonderful online sites available now (like Caringbridge) that allow family and friends to receive updates on your loved one's condition. Encourage them to check your posts, as it will relieve you of the necessity of repeating the same information multiple times.

• Caller ID on your phone is a helpful tool to protect you from an onslaught of well-meaning family and friends who want to know the latest news by phone. When Bethany was ill, my energy was so sapped it was all I could do some days to take care of her. I couldn't take care of everyone else by giving constant updates. When Steve was home, I told him who was on my list of callers with whom I could speak. That way if he chose, he could answer the phone but give excuses for me.

• Do not be afraid to change doctors if you are not satisfied with the care your loved one is receiving. Ask for a referral from a doctor you trust. When a serious illness is involved, you may have a huge number of physicians to whom you are "assigned." Not all doctors are the right fit.

• Keep a list of folks who have volunteered to help and include their phone numbers.

• Be prepared for acquaintances to offer miracle cures along the way. Some of these could perhaps be useful but most will likely be hype. And they will most likely not be a miracle cure. Ask for research and why this person knows they are a miracle. I have seen friends promote such fix-alls at the most inappropriate times — like when the patient is dying. Be prepared — and be ready to forgive.

• Do not neglect your own health and emotional wellbeing. You may be eating on the run a great deal. If you don't already take vitamin supplements, this may be the time to start. A quality multi-vitamin plus a B-Complex with zinc (for stress) is a starting place. Do some form of exercise at least three days a week. If you are ill, you cannot help your patient.

• Be aware that many times, the people who you think would be the most supportive and helpful, will let you down in one way or another. If there are friends or family who are draining you of emotional energy, it is okay to keep them at a distance until you are capable of dealing with them. You are the caregiver and your patient is your priority. I would encourage you to forgive those people. They are hurting as well.

This is perhaps the most difficult advice to offer…

• If your loved one is dying, pray that God will give you the strength to talk to him or her about healthcare wishes. You can be designated as their medical Power of Attorney if they reach a point one day where they can no longer let their desires be known. Check with your doctor's office about obtaining formal documentation.

• Discuss final arrangements. Who would they like to officiate at their funeral? What songs would he or she want played? Any special requests?

These are the most difficult conversations you may ever initiate. But if your loved one is dying, they likely know it, and will be grateful you brought it up. And it will give you, the caregiver who loves them, the knowledge that you gave them a final farewell of their choosing. This will give you immense peace, despite your grief.

May the Lord bless you and bring you *His* comfort and peace.

ELAINE MARIE COOPER

Novelist Elaine Marie Cooper is the author of *Fields of the Fatherless* and the Deer Run saga (*The Road to Deer Run, The Promise of Deer Run* and *The Legacy of Deer Run*.) Her passions are her family, her faith in Christ, and the history of the American Revolution, a frequent subject of her historical fiction. She grew up in Massachusetts, the setting for many of her novels.

Elaine is a contributing writer to *Fighting Fear, Winning the War at Home* by Edie Melson, and *I Choose You*, a romance anthology. Her freelance work has appeared in both newspapers and magazines, and she blogs regularly at ColonialQuills.blogspot.com as well as her own blog on her website at ElaineMarieCooper.com.

www.ElaineMarieCooper.com
www.Facebook.com/ElaineMarieCooperAuthor
www.Twitter.com/ElaineMCooper

MORE ENCOURAGING BOOKS
FROM CROSSRIVERMEDIA.COM

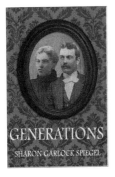

GENERATIONS
Sharon Garlock Spiegel

When Edward Garlock was sober, he was a kind, generous, hard-working farmer, providing for his wife and growing family. But when he drank, he transformed into a unpredictable bully, capable of absolute cruelty. When he stepped into a revival tent in the early 1900s the Holy Spirit got ahold of him, changing not only his life, but the future of thousands of others through Edward.

CONFESSIONS OF A LIP READING MOM
Shanna Groves

As she held her newborn son, Shanna Groves should have reveled in the joys of motherhood. Instead, she was plagued by questions and fear. Something was terribly wrong. The sounds she once took for granted were gone, replaced by silence. Then the buzzing started. In *Confessions of a Lip Reading Mom*, Shanna shares her struggle to find God's grace during her roller coaster ride of unexplained deafness.

THE GRACE IMPACT
Nancy Kay Grace

The promise of grace pulses throughout Scripture. Chapter after chapter, the Bible shows a loving heavenly Father lavishing his grace on us through His son. In her book, *The Grace Impact*, author Nancy Kay Grace gives us a closer glimpse at God's character. His grace covers every detail of life, not just the good things, but the difficult, sad, and complicated things. That knowledge can give us the ability to walk confidently through life knowing God is with us every step of the way.

17039591R00097

Made in the USA
San Bernardino, CA
28 November 2014